The Stature of Waiting

# The Stature of Waiting

W. H. VANSTONE

The Seabury Press · New York

1983
The Seabury Press
815 Second Avenue
New York, N.Y. 10017

Published in Great Britain by Darton, Longman & Todd Ltd.

Printed in the United States of America


**Library of Congress Cataloging in Publication Data**

Vanstone, W. H. (William Hubert)
The stature of waiting.

1. Jesus Christ—Betrayal. 2. Christian life—
Anglican authors. I. Title.
BT435.V36 1983      232.9′61      83-4241
ISBN 0-8164-2478-0 (pbk.)

*Hunc cui et alterum*
*grato animo*
*dedico librum*

# Contents

# Preface

This book is a small and limited exercise in what Paul Tillich called the method of correlation—a method which he thought appropriate to theology, which he taught to his students and which he himself followed with so great distinction. The method implies that there is a dialectical relationship between divine revelation and human perception: that what we are 'told' in revelation is only understood in the light of our perception of the world around us, while at the same time our perception of the world is itself illuminated by the light of revelation.

Some time ago I turned my mind to a small factual puzzle in the story of Jesus which had bothered me from childhood. Gradually through attention to the puzzle I detected a certain emphasis running through the story, and through the emphasis a theme—a theme which seemed to resonate with certain quite ordinary facts and experiences of contemporary life. To define that resonance, to identify and draw out a particular thread of connection between the story of Jesus and the way we see the world today is the purpose of the pages which follow.

The argument is set out more or less in the sequence in which it developed in my own mind. It did not develop easily, and many times I found myself straying into by-ways or tracing my steps back from dead ends. Groups who heard parts or facets of the argument were encouraging, and I am grateful to them. But nothing coherent would ever have emerged but for the interest and encouragement of three old and trusted friends—Bishop Victor Whitsey, Canon David

Wyatt and Mr Michael Daman. Each in his own particular way helped me to believe that I was not following a Will-o'-the-Wisp or searching for a mare's nest; and I am very deeply grateful.

My warm thanks go also to the Dean and Canons of Chester for allowing me time to think, and to my publishers, Messrs Darton, Longman and Todd, for bearing with my many procrastinations.

W. H. Vanstone
Chester 1982

# 1

# The Deed of Judas

A generation or so ago it was the custom in many churches to arrange in Lent or Holy Week a series of sermons with some such title as 'Characters Round the Cross' or 'Actors in the Drama of the Passion'. A preacher or a number of different preachers would invite the congregation to reflect on the characters of certain people, on their strengths and weaknesses, and on the part which they played in the last days of Jesus—such people as Simon Peter, Pontius Pilate, Barabbas the Robber, Simon of Cyrene, Mary of Magdala and, invariably, Judas Iscariot. When I was young I listened to a good many sermons about Judas Iscariot.

The details of these sermons about Judas have long since faded from my memory. But a general impression remains that the preachers were principally concerned with the *motives* of Judas in doing what he did. One preacher would be content to represent him in the traditional way as a man in whom the love of money had become dominant over every other motive. Another would put forward the suggestion that Judas' principal motive may have been a certain resentment at his exclusion from that trio—Peter, James and John—who formed the 'inner circle' of Jesus' associates. A third would suggest that Judas, an able man, may have become irritated by Jesus' apparent failure to take the opportunities which were offered to Him; and that such irritation, deepening into disillusionment and bitterness, may have been Judas' primary motive in doing what he did. Some of these suggestions and explanations were no doubt rather speculative, but often, to the best of my recollection, they were quite interestingly pre-

1

sented. At least they reminded the hearers that, as Dostoevsky puts it in *The Idiot*: 'The causes of human actions are usually immeasurably more complex than are our subsequent explanations of them, and can rarely be distinctly discerned.'

But I also remember that, even when I was young, most of these sermons about Judas left me somewhat dissatisfied. I felt let down because they did not answer, or even ask, a question which seemed to me very important. It was the question whether the deed of Judas had any actual effect on the course of events: whether it really mattered and, if so, in what way it mattered. The preachers all seemed to assume that it mattered a great deal, for they used of Judas such phrases as 'he sent his Master to His death', 'he had Jesus' blood on his hands', 'through his greed or resentment or disillusionment he became guilty of the greatest crime in history'. But for myself I could not see that this was in fact the case. I could see of course that Judas had done a very shameful deed—a deed at least as shameful as that which Peter did when he denied that he knew Jesus or that which the other disciples did when they forsook Jesus and fled from the Garden of Gethsemane—a deed perhaps even more shameful for being premeditated. But I could not see that this deed of Judas had been of any great importance, that it had had any decisive consequences or any major effect on the course of events during that Passover season in Jerusalem.

For it seemed to me then, as it still seems to me now, that if Judas had done nothing at all events would still have taken much the same course. The deed of Judas was by no means necessary to bring about the arrest of Jesus and to set in train the sequence of events which ended in His crucifixion. For it appears from the Gospels, which are our only evidence, that in His last days in Jerusalem Jesus did not live in hiding or move around secretly as the Scarlet Pimpernel moved around Paris—a man of many disguises who could only be arrested by his enemies if He were first identified to them by a traitor among His friends. Jesus could not be betrayed as many an escaped prisoner or underground agent was, or might have been, betrayed in the last war. For it appears that Jesus lived

2

quite openly and that His opponents or their representatives could find Him without difficulty when they wished to hear or criticize His teaching or to pose hard questions to Him. Presumably, therefore, they could have found Him with no greater difficulty if and when they wanted to arrest Him. Admittedly it might have been indiscreet to attempt an arrest when He was surrounded by crowds of attentive and perhaps enthusiastic pilgrims from Galilee; but it was surely not beyond the capacity of politicians and scheming priests to have Him 'shadowed' by some of their own men and a report brought of His whereabouts when He was more or less alone. What Judas offered to do may have been welcomed as a convenience by the opponents of Jesus, but it can hardly have been regarded as a necessity. So if Judas had made no offer the last events of the life of Jesus would have proceeded in very much the same way. Judas' deed was certainly shameful; but it did no more to change the course of history or to bring about the death of Jesus than did Peter's denial or the somnolence of the three disciples who were set to watch in the Garden of Gethsemane or the later flight of the whole band.

Yet the preachers of my youth, by branding Judas with so much responsibility for the death of Jesus, represented his deed as of major importance in the development of events. This seemed to me unreasonable, and I came to the private conclusion that the preachers, in order to warn us against the vices of greed or resentment, were somewhat exaggerating the dreadful consequences of these vices as they had appeared in Judas.

In later years, however, when I came to have a rather better knowledge of the Gospels, I realized that the preachers, if not wholly justified in what they said, were at least consistent with the Gospels. For the Gospel writers themselves give the impression that the deed of Judas was no mere peripheral incident in their story but was an event of major importance. John, who often assumes a good deal of background knowledge on the part of his readers, tells us no fewer than five times what it was that Judas did; and the other three Evangelists give equal prominence to his deed. All four

3

Gospels report Jesus' ominous words at the Last Supper about this impending deed and the perpetrator of it; and all four writers, on their first mention of Judas in the early stages of their story, give, as it were, advance notice of what he did in the last stage. When this last stage is reached, all four make reference at significant points to what Judas was doing or planning. The last stage, normally called the Passion narrative, falls in each of the Gospels into two sections—the first dealing with the Last Supper and what was said and done in the course of it, the second narrating the sequence of events from the arrest of Jesus to His death—and we notice that in each of the Gospels each of these sections begins with a mention of the actions or designs of Judas. It is rather as if, in a narrative of the downfall of Hitler, a historian should preface his account of each critical event—the Battle of Stalingrad, the Desert War, the invasion of Europe—with a reference to the defection of Rudolph Hess. We should certainly conclude from this that, in the historian's view, the defection of Hess had a decisive bearing on the fate of Hitler. Similarly, from the significance of those moments at which Judas is mentioned in the later stages of all the Gospels, we are led to conclude that, in the Evangelists' view, his deed was of major importance in the development of events.

And yet, as we have seen, that deed cannot have been of major importance in a strictly historical sense: it cannot in itself have determined or changed the course of events. It began to seem to me, therefore, that the Gospel writers might be representing the deed of Judas as important in something other than a strictly historical sense: as important in a symbolic or theological sense: as important not in accounting for what happened in the last hours of Jesus' life but in expressing the meaning of what happened. I began to think that, in the eyes of the Gospel writers, the deed of Judas might be important as a symbol of something which was going on, as it were, behind the scenes or at a deeper level.

I had reached this stage of reflection when I began to notice some curious features about the actual words in which the deed of Judas is described in all the Gospels. I was so familiar

4

with the phrases referring to Judas in our English versions of the Scripture—that he 'betrayed' Jesus and that he was a 'traitor'—that it came as a surprise when I realized that, except in one instance, these phrases are almost certainly mistranslations of the original Greek. The English verb 'betray' implies or suggests ill will, unfaithfulness and secrecy on the part of the person who betrays, and loss, tragedy or hardship for the person who is betrayed: and the Greek equivalent for this verb is *prodidōmi*. Now there are twenty-two occasions in the New Testament on which the deed of Judas is mentioned, and another eleven occasions on which the deed is mentioned but is attributed to 'one of the Twelve' or 'one of you' rather than specifically to Judas. And among all these thirty-three occasions there is only one—that is in Luke's list of the Twelve Disciples—on which the deed is described by the verb *prodidōmi* (or, more exactly, by the noun *prodotēs* or 'traitor', which is derived from the verb). So on only one occasion in the New Testament is it said that Judas 'betrayed' Jesus. On one other occasion an exceptional and unique phrase is used to describe what Judas did—that is in Peter's speech at the beginning of the Acts of the Apostles when he refers to Judas as 'the guide to those who arrested Jesus'. On the other thirty-one occasions in which the deed of Judas is referred to it is always described in the same way—by some part of the Greek verb *paradidōmi*.

A reader who is unfamiliar with Greek should not be misled by the seemingly small difference between *prodidōmi* and *paradidōmi*. They have, of course, the same stem in the verb *didōmi* —'to give'; but the different prefixes produce quite different ranges of meaning. So it is with such a pair of English words as 'receive' and 'deceive'. Both verbs have the same stem—the Latin *capio* meaning 'to take'; but the two different prefixes generate a wide difference of meaning. So it is with *prodidōmi* and *paradidōmi*. *Prodidōmi*, as we have seen, is properly translated 'to betray': let us now illustrate the meaning of *paradidōmi*. Let us pick out some of the many passages in which the verb is used in the New Testament in contexts which have nothing to do with Judas, and, in order to avoid the need to repeat the verb each time in its Greek form, let us translate it on each occasion by the fairly colourless English phrase 'to hand over'.

When John describes the death of Jesus on the Cross, he says that Jesus 'bowed His head and handed over His spirit'. When Luke describes the departure of Paul on a missionary journey, he says that Paul 'was handed over to the grace of God by the brethren'. When Paul refers to his preaching of the Gospel to the Corinthians, he says that 'he handed over to them' that which he had himself received. It is quite evident that in such passages as these *paradidōmi* could not possibly be translated as 'betray'. There is no suggestion that the person who hands over does so in ill will, unfaithfulness or secrecy; nor that the person who, or the thing which, is handed over is destined for loss or tragedy or hardship. Rather, in fact, the reverse. In these particular cases 'to be handed over' is to pass into good hands, with the likelihood of being cared for and preserved. In other contexts the case is different—as when, at the end of the parable of the Unmerciful Servant, that servant is 'handed over to the tormentors', or when Paul decrees that a notorious evil-liver at Corinth shall be 'handed over to Satan for the destruction of his flesh'. In these contexts, although the translation 'betray' would be just as inappropriate as elsewhere, there is present an implication that there will be loss, tragedy or hardship for the person who is handed over; but the implication comes not from the verb *paradidōmi* itself but from the total context, including the kind of hands—the tormentor's hands, Satan's hands—into which the person is to pass. The verb *paradidōmi* itself is ambivalent, neutral, colourless. Perhaps the most revealing illustration of its meaning is to be found in the parable of the Talents. There the householder hands over his eight talents to three servants, of whom two make good use of what is handed over to them and one makes bad use. The destiny—good or bad—of the talents depends entirely on the response of those who receive them: neither a good destiny nor a bad is implied in the fact that they are 'handed over'.

So the word which is normally used in the Gospels of the

deed of Judas is ambivalent, neutral, colourless. One may well wonder how it is that in the Authorized Version of the Bible—which in its turn has influenced all later translations— this neutral word came to be translated by the emotively loaded and pejorative word 'betray'. Probably the reason lies in the influence on the translators of their familiarity with the Latin version of the Bible—the Vulgate. The Latin verb *trado* is a correct translation of both *prodidōmi* and *paradidōmi*: it has a range of meaning which covers both Greek verbs, a range so broad that it has generated in English words with such diverse meanings as 'traitor' and 'tradition'. We must suppose that the sixteenth- and seventeenth-century translators, having understood *trado* in the Vulgate as 'betray' and Judas the *traditor* as the 'traitor', brought this presupposition with them when they came to translate the Greek verb *paradidōmi*; and so read into this word a loaded and pejorative significance which, as we have seen, it does not in fact possess. This erroneous presupposition of the early English translators—namely, that the Gospel writers themselves normally call the deed of Judas a 'betrayal' and Judas himself a 'traitor'—has probably had a subconscious influence on all later translators.

Whatever the reason for the familiar mistranslation of *paradidōmi*, as 'betray', it remains a mistranslation. The verb is ambivalent, neutral, colourless; and we shall continue to translate it as 'to hand over'.

Now it is surely remarkable that all the four Evangelists should normally use so colourless a word to describe what Judas did. For they show no love for Judas, nor any tendency to play down the evil of his character or the gravity of his offence. They say, in various passages, that he was a thief, that the concern which he professed for the poor was a pretence, that he was inspired by Satan, and that he was himself a devil; and Peter's words about Judas reported at the beginning of the Acts of the Apostles are almost literally damnatory. We should expect, therefore, that in referring to what Judas did the Evangelists would use the harshest, most derogatory word that was available. The word *prodidōmi* —

7

'betray'—was certainly available; for, as we have noticed, it is used once by Luke. We should therefore expect that this word, or some word or phrase equally derogatory, would be the normal expression of the writers of the Gospels. But in fact they use it only once, and in thirty-one instances out of thirty-three make use of the neutral and ambivalent *paradidōmi*. It is as if four newspaper reporters, telling how a father murdered his infant son by dropping him from a high window, should all, on the one hand, refer to the father as a 'brute', a 'monster' or a 'devil', but should all, on the other hand, speak of him not as 'dropping', 'throwing' or 'flinging' the infant from the window but as 'releasing' him. We should certainly find such a manner of reporting the incident surprising.

It is remarkable that the neutral *paradidōmi* should ever be used in the Gospels of the deed of Judas; it is much more remarkable that it should be used so consistently. We have noticed that once, in the Acts of the Apostles, it is said that Judas was 'guide to those who arrested Jesus', and this expression may suggest other ways in which Judas and his deed might naturally have been described. The deed might have been described as that of 'selling Jesus for money' or 'assisting His enemies' or 'planning His arrest'; and Judas might have been called 'the false friend', 'the secret enemy', 'the informer' and so on. Phrases such as these fell readily from the lips of the preachers of my youth, but from the Gospels they are entirely and strikingly absent. Time after time the deed is that of 'handing Jesus over' and Judas himself is 'the hander-over'. Anyone who is reasonably familiar with the New Testament knows that, if the same incident or the same thing is described in different Gospels, then—unless one of the writers is following another so closely as to be transcribing from him—there are normally verbal differences between the various passages. So, for instance, each of the Gospels has a slightly different version of the wording of that notice which was pinned upon the Cross, and in each a different phrase is used to describe Jesus' actual death. Three different words are used in the Gospels of the tomb in which His body was

8

laid; the instrument of His death, normally called in the New Testament the 'Cross' ( *stauros* ), is occasionally referred to as the 'Tree' (*xulon*); and two different words are used almost indiscriminately to describe His rising from death. So even over such central facts and incidents in the life of Jesus the language of the Gospels is not so uniform and consistent as it is in descriptions of the deed of Judas. Indeed it would be hard to find a parallel in the New Testament for such consistency of expression as appears in reference to the deed of Judas. Judas is more frequently and consistently the 'hander-over' than John the son of Zacharias is 'the baptizer': indeed on several occasions he appears simply as 'the hander-over' without mention of his name. And so closely is the verb 'to hand over' associated with Judas that on one occasion Matthew attaches it to him in a phrase which hardly makes sense. This is the occasion on which Judas attempts to return the Thirty Pieces of Silver to the Jewish leaders. 'I have sinned,' says Judas, 'in that I have handed over innocent blood.' What presumably Judas means is that he has *shed* innocent blood; but the name of Judas seems to 'attract' the verb *paradidōmi* so powerfully that Matthew uses it almost instinctively and so produces a phrase which defies literal translation and compels the authors of the New English Bible to resort to a paraphrase.

With a consistency for which there seems to be no parallel in the New Testament, the Gospel writers use, in almost ninety-five per cent of their many references to the deed of Judas, one particular word—the verb *paradidōmi* and the word is by no means the kind of derogatory or offensive word which we should expect from writers who thought so very ill of Judas. Here is a remarkable fact which calls for thought and explanation.

A simple explanation which suggests itself is that, in their references to Judas, the Gospel writers are simply using the particular word which Jesus Himself used when, at the Last Supper, He forewarned His disciples of the deed which was to be done—whether by 'one of the Twelve' or, explicitly, by Judas. Now we know, of course, that the words which Jesus

9

spoke even at such crucial moments as the institution of the Eucharist, His trial before Pilate and His dying upon the Cross tend to be rather differently reported by different Evangelists. But it might be argued that in this particular case Jesus' words of warning were so shocking and unexpected that they caused a *frisson* of horror round the supper table, and that, in consequence, His exact words on that occasion became indelibly imprinted in the minds of those who heard them and firmly fixed in the memory and tradition of the early Church. But this explanation, simplistic rather than simple, is not satisfactory. Jesus spoke not Greek but Aramaic. If He used at the Last Supper an Aramaic word as shocking and ominous as the English word 'betray'—if He really pointed to 'treachery' in the inner circle—then why was the ill-omened and appalling word which He then used translated into Greek by the neutral and colourless *paradidōmi*? If on the other hand He used an Aramaic word as ambivalent as *paradidōmi*, what reason was there for such shock and horror as would make an indelible impression? There would rather have been uncertainty and puzzled faces; and the immediate question would not have been 'Whom does He mean?' but '*What* does He mean?' The phrase 'one of you will hand me over' is by no means the kind of phrase which would make an unforgettable impact and leave an indelible impression. It is a phrase requiring further explanation—a phrase so ambiguous in its meaning as to be, in itself, more puzzling than shocking.

The remarkable fact which we have noticed—the remarkable consistency with which all the Evangelists use of Judas and his deed a word which would scarcely represent their own revulsion to what he had done—requires deeper reflection. In my own reflection on the problem the first glimmer of light appeared when I observed that it is not by Judas only that Jesus is said to have been handed over. There are two other contexts in the Gospels in which the verb *paradidōmi* appears with Jesus as the object but with subjects other than Judas; and in each of these contexts its appearance is slightly surprising. Let us consider these two contexts.

Luke writes that, when the Jewish leaders had questioned Jesus and satisfied themselves 'out of His own mouth' that He was guilty of blasphemy, they took Him and accused Him to, or before, Pontius Pilate. To Pilate they accused Him not of blasphemy but of political disaffection; but the point to be noticed is simply that, according to Luke, they *accused* Him to Pilate. However, at the same point in the story, Matthew and Mark say that they 'handed Jesus over' to Pilate; and John implies the same when he reports the Jewish leaders as saying, 'If this man were not a wrong-doer, we should not have handed Him over to you'. Now the suggestion of Matthew, Mark and John that the Jewish leaders 'handed Jesus over' to Pilate does not seem entirely appropriate. It implies that the Jewish leaders gave to Pilate some right or power or permission, which he would not otherwise have possessed, to deal with Jesus; and, furthermore, that they left the matter in Pilate's hands to decide and deal with as he thought fit. But this was by no means the actual situation. The power of a Roman governor to take judicial or punitive action—at least in the case of someone who was not a Roman citizen—certainly did not depend on the mandate or permission of the local authorities. He might hand over an accused or suspected wrong-doer to them; but they could hardly be said to 'hand over' a wrong-doer to him. Every suspected wrong-doer was already, so to speak, in his hands. Furthermore it was clearly not the case that the Jewish authorities were willing to 'leave the matter in Pilate's hands': they were determined on a verdict of 'guilty' and a sentence of execution. So the use of the verb *paradidōmi* at this point by Matthew, Mark and John seems slightly inappropriate. Without overstating the case we may say that Luke's expression—'they accused Jesus to Pilate'—is distinctly more appropriate at this point than that of the other three Evangelists: but it is the less appropriate expression, involving the use of *paradidōmi*, which predominates.

The second context to be noticed is the end of the trial of Jesus before Pilate. No Gospel writer reports that Pilate 'found Jesus guilty' or 'condemned Him to death' or 'ordered

11

Him to be crucified': all report that he 'handed Him over to be crucified', or 'handed Him over to them', or 'handed Him over to their will'. The word *paradidōmi* is not of course inappropriate here, but it is by no means the only appropriate word by which to report what Pilate decided and did. It is a little surprising, therefore, that it should appear at this point in all four of the Gospels, and the more so since the actual sequence of events is rather differently represented at this point in different Gospels. In Matthew and Mark the soldiers come into the story here, taking Jesus away from Pilate's presence to dress Him in the purple robe and pay mock homage; so it is in effect to the soldiers that Jesus is handed over by Pilate. But in the other two Gospels there is no mention of the soldiers at this stage. It is 'to them'—those who have demanded His crucifixion—that Jesus is handed over, or to 'their will', and it is 'they' who forthwith lead Him away from Pilate to Calvary. The sequence of events is slightly different in different Gospels, and different figures respond to Pilate's decision. But in all the Gospels the report of that decision involves the use of the same phrase: 'he handed Jesus over'.

In these two contexts the verb *paradidōmi*, with Jesus as its object, appears where we should not quite expect it, or at least more frequently than we should expect it. The verb seems, as it were, to demand a place in the story: to intrude: to suggest itself to the writers, or even force itself upon them, as a word which *must* be used in this later stage of the story of Jesus. From the two contexts which we have examined we get the impression that, at the least, the word came very readily to the mind of anyone who, in telling the story of Jesus, had reached the later stages.

There is perhaps here the beginning of a solution to that problem with which we have been concerned—the problem of the prominence given in the Gospels to the historically unimportant deed of Judas, of the ambivalent word which is used to describe this base deed, and of the remarkable consistency with which this word is used. Let us suppose for a moment that, before ever the Gospels were written, the phrase

12

'He was handed over' was widely used in Christian circles to express the meaning of Jesus and the benefit which He had brought to the believers. Let us suppose that when Christians wanted to say what it was, in all that they knew about Jesus, that mattered most and was most important to them, they said that 'He was handed over' or that 'He was handed over for our sake'. If this were the case, then when the story of Jesus came to be written in the Gospels, the phrase 'He was handed over' would, so to speak, cry aloud for a niche, for a place in the historical narrative. Any incident in the narrative, such as Pilate's verdict, which *could* be represented as a 'handing over of Jesus' *would* be so represented; and the shameful but historically unimportant deed of Judas would provide a particularly appropriate niche for the use of the highly significant, highly resonant phrase. Hence the prominence given to the deed: it was an appropriate context for the all-important phrase; Judas himself was an appropriate subject for the all-important verb. The Evangelists' own feelings about Judas would have suggested a harsher, more opprobrious description of what he did; but any other description would have lacked the resonance and suggestiveness for Christian ears of the fact that by the deed of Judas Jesus was, in a physical and historical sense, 'handed over'. Except as the subject of that particular verb Judas had no major place in, or relevance to, the story: except as 'the handing over of Jesus' his shameful deed was of no more than peripheral importance. It was the phrase 'Jesus was handed over' that must be prominent in the story; the deed of Judas owes its prominence to the fact that it was an appropriate context for that phrase.

So the supposition which we have made enables us to explain certain puzzling facts about the Gospel stories—the prominence given to Judas and his deed, the ambivalent phrase in which the deed is described, and the remarkable consistency with which the phrase is used. But the supposition is in fact more than a supposition. There is concrete evidence in the writings of Paul that, before ever the Gospels were written, Christians were using the phrase 'Jesus was handed over' to point to the heart and core of His meaning to the

13

believer and of the benefit received by the believer from or through Him. Three passages of Paul's writings are particularly significant in this respect.

If someone reasonably familiar with Paul's writings were asked to select two sentences which express most fervently and concisely the Apostle's gratitude to and for Jesus and his heartfelt appreciation of the benefit received through Jesus, he might well select one passage from the Epistle to the Galatians and one from the Epistle to the Romans. The fervour and eloquence of Paul's words is perhaps best caught in the Authorized Version of the Scripture; and it is from this version that we quote. The sentence from Galatians reads: 'The life which I now live in the flesh I live by the faith of the Son of God, Who loved me and gave Himself for me.' But the word translated as 'gave' is in fact this very verb *paradidōmi*, with which we have been so much concerned, and we might well translate '. . . Who loved me and handed Himself over for me'. The sentence from Romans reads: 'He that spared not His own Son but delivered Him up for us all, how shall He not also with Him freely give us all things?' But the verb translated as 'delivered up' is again *paradidōmi*, and we might well translate, 'He that spared not His own Son but handed Him over for us all. . . .' In both of these passages the Son of God is said to be 'handed over'—not indeed by Judas, but in the first case by His own will and in the second case by the will of the Father. Nevertheless He is seen and described as 'handed over', and the fact that He is handed over is the focus of the Apostle's gratitude.

The other passage of Paul's writings which is significant in this connection is that in his First Epistle to the Corinthians in which he tries to correct certain misunderstandings of his readers about the meaning of the Eucharist and certain improprieties in their own conduct of it. Paul refers in these words to his own teaching on the matter when he was in Corinth: 'I received from the Lord that which I also handed over to you—that the Lord Jesus, on the night in which He was handed over, took bread and, having given thanks, broke it and said . . .' Now when Paul writes that he had received this account 'from the Lord' he can hardly mean that he had received it personally from Jesus and in Jesus' own words: his meaning must presumably be that this account goes back to the Lord, and it is by no means Paul's private and personal interpretation but is accepted in the Church as the authentic version of what actually took place. So we notice that, in what seems to be the accepted teaching, phraseology or formula of the Church, the night of the institution of the Eucharist is identified as 'the night in which Jesus was handed over'. It might with equal precision have been identified as 'the night in which He was arrested', 'the night before He died', 'the last night of His life'. But in fact, in connection with the very important matter of the institution of the Eucharist, reference is once again made to 'the handing over' of Jesus; and it appears that this reference was made not only in the private reflection of Paul but in what was—so far as anything could be at that date—the accepted teaching and phraseology of the Church. It is clear therefore that it was not Paul alone who thought and spoke of Jesus as 'handed over': the expression was familiar and significant in the Church at large before the Gospels were written.

So the supposition or hypothesis which was necessary to solve the problems connected with the deed of Judas proves to have independent evidence in its favour. It seems reasonably certain that the phrase 'the handing over of Jesus' was familiar to the Christians of the first generation, and so significant to them that it had its effect on the manner in which the later part of the story of Jesus was narrated in the Gospels: in particular it led the writers to give prominence to that squalid deed of Judas which, though it had little bearing on the actual course of events, was, in a physical and historical sense, a 'handing over' of Jesus.

So the phrase, and the concept expressed in the phrase, was clearly important to the early Christians. But what exactly did it mean to them? As we have seen, the verb *paradidōmi* is, in itself, a neutral, ambivalent word: it may mean, according to its context, anything from 'entrust' to 'condemn', anything from passing a precious possession into trusted

15

hands to abandoning a loathsome person to the devil. What had the early Christians in mind when they used this phrase of Jesus? What in their view was effected or changed when Jesus was handed over? How did they 'see' Him before and after He was handed over? If we can answer this kind of question we shall be in a better position to understand what Paul and others mean when they declared, with fervent gratitude, that Jesus had been handed over for them.

In an attempt to answer the question we shall look rather closely at what actually happens in the Gospel story when Jesus is handed over. As we have noticed, Jesus is said to be handed over on three different occasions and by three different subjects—by Judas in the Garden of Gethsemane, by the Jewish leaders at Pilate's tribunal and by Pilate at the end of the trial. But it is the event in the Garden which is most frequently and consistently referred to as the handing-over of Jesus: it is Judas who is the hander-over *par excellence* and bears that title. The later actions of the Jewish leaders and of Pilate are as it were ripples or echoes of the decisive handover by the deed of Judas. So it is at the moment of that deed and event in the Garden that we must look in order to discover what actually happens when Jesus is handed over. We shall pursue the inquiry in the two archetypal Gospels—those of Mark and John; and, as Socrates recommended, we shall attempt to follow the evidence and the argument 'whithersoever it may lead'.

# 2

# The Handing Over of Jesus

In order to perceive what happens in Mark's Gospel when Jesus is handed over in the Garden, in order to detect any change which comes about at that point, we must begin much earlier in the Gospel. In fact we must begin at the beginning of the Gospel—or, more exactly, at the ninth verse of the first chapter, where Jesus first appears, coming from Nazareth to be baptized by John. It has often been noticed that in the remainder of the chapter the Greek word meaning 'straightway' or 'immediately' occurs no less than eleven times. The writer gives the impression that, from the moment when Jesus appeared in public, events followed rapidly one upon another. Although the word 'immediately' appears less frequently after the first chapter, the impression continues that events were moving at a brisk pace. Mark's manner is to give a brief description of a scene or situation; then to report an action or comment which decisively changed that situation; then, after the briefest reference to the change in the situation, to pass on quite abruptly to a new scene or incident. The pace of events is brisk in Mark's Gospel: the narrative has a vigorous momentum.

It is the activity of Jesus which maintains the momentum. He is constantly moving from place to place, from situation to situation; and always it is His intervention in word or deed which changes the situation. So as He moves about He leaves behind Him a trail of transformed scenes and changed situations—fishermen no longer at their nets, sick people restored to health, critics confounded, a storm stilled, hunger assuaged, a dead girl raised to life. Jesus' presence is an active and instantly transforming presence: He is never the mere observer of the scene or the one who waits upon events but always the transformer of the scene and the initiator of events. It is interesting to note in detail how much activity on the part of Jesus Mark will—no doubt unconsciously—write into an episode which one would imagine to have been, in fact, a rather quiet episode, an occasion of reflection rather than of action. In his account of Jesus' appointment of the Twelve Disciples, Mark makes Jesus the grammatical subject of seven verbs within six lines of the Greek text:

> *He went up* the mountain and *He called* those whom *He wished*, and they came to Him. And *He appointed* twelve that they might be with Him and that *He might send* them to preach and to cast out devils. And *He gave* to Simon the name Peter; and to James the son of Zebedee and John the brother of James *He gave* the name Boanerges.

Similarly in his account of the famous conversation between Jesus and His disciples at Caesarea Philippi—an account occupying no more than fourteen lines—he writes that Jesus *came*; twice that *He asked*; twice that *He rebuked*; that *He began to teach*; that *He spoke freely*; that *He turned*; that *He saw* the disciples; that *He spoke* to Peter; that *He called* the crowd; and that *He spoke* to the crowd. Here in the fourteen lines Jesus is the grammatical subject of twelve verbs: it is His activity which carries the episode forward and sustains its momentum.

The impression which Mark gives of constant activity on the part of Jesus is accentuated by two characteristics of his manner or style of writing. In the first place, he has a tendency to report scenes and situations through Jesus' eyes or from Jesus' point of view. So he writes not that 'Simon and Andrew were casting their nets' but that 'Jesus saw them casting their nets': not that 'the Spirit descended as a dove' but that 'Jesus saw the Spirit descending': not that 'Levi was sitting at the receipt of custom' but that 'Jesus saw him sitting there'. Instances of this characteristic of Marcan style are very numerous; and, as well as seeing things through Jesus' eyes, Mark very often attributes to the activity of Jesus things which other people did and situations in which other people were placed. So he does not write that Peter, James and John went with Jesus up the Mount of the Transfiguration but that Jesus *took them* with Him up the Mount. He does not write that the same three fell asleep in the Garden of Gethsemane but that Jesus *found them* sleeping. Mark's account of the Feeding of the Four Thousand ends not with the crowd going away but with Jesus *letting them go*; and the next episode, a visit by some questioning Pharisees, ends not in their departure but in Jesus' *dismissal* of them. Mark so writes that many things done by other people are presented, at least in a grammatical sense, as the outcome of Jesus' activity and initiative.

The second characteristic of Mark's style which tends to emphasize the activity of Jesus is his habit of frequently making mention of Jesus' *inner* activity of thought and feeling. Mark does not leave us to deduce Jesus' thoughts and feelings from His outward activities: he tells us explicitly what they were. A few out of many instances will suffice to make the point. Mark tells us not only that Jesus, seeing a large crowd of people, began to teach them, but also that He *had compassion* on them because they were as sheep without a shepherd; not only that His mighty works were inhibited by the unbelief of the people of Nazareth but also that He *wondered* at their unbelief; not only that He looked round when a woman, in search of healing, touched His garment, but also that He did so because He *knew* that power had gone out of Him. In passages where the reader might easily deduce the thoughts and feelings of Jesus from what He said or did, Mark draws attention explicitly to these thoughts and feelings; and so he conveys a strong impression that the story he is telling is not that of certain events which took place in first-century Palestine but, primarily and overwhelmingly, the story of the activity and initiative and decisiveness of Jesus.

Now this characteristic of Mark's manner of telling the story is not perhaps remarkable in itself: to some extent it is a normal characteristic of the biographical manner. A biography of Churchill may well give the impression that the conduct of the Western Allies in the Second World War consisted, primarily and overwhelmingly, of the actions and intentions, the hopes and fears, of Winston Churchill. What is remarkable in Mark's Gospel is the change of manner of which we become aware at a certain point in the narrative; and this is the point at which Jesus is handed over by Judas in the Garden. The change of manner consists in this—that from this point to the moment of Jesus' death on the Cross, a period which occupies, in Souter's text, one hundred lines of narrative, Jesus is the grammatical subject of just nine verbs. And the reason for the change is not, of course, that Mark has now gone on to a different story and that Jesus is no longer there. Jesus is there all the time, at the very centre of the story. But now He is no longer there as the active and initiating subject of what is done: He is there as the recipient, the object, of what is done.

Let us look at the matter in some detail. From the moment when Jesus is handed over in the Garden, Mark reports no single incident through Jesus' eyes and attributes nothing that happens to His initiative and activity. Whereas previously Mark has told us freely of what Jesus felt among the sceptical people of Nazareth and of what He thought when a woman touched the hem of His garment, now He tells us nothing whatever of what Jesus thought or felt, or of how He reacted, inwardly or outwardly, to what was done to Him. Preachers often tell us of the courage and patience of Jesus during His trial and crucifixion: and no doubt what they say is correct. But they cannot have learned what they say from Mark's Gospel. For Mark writes no single word about Jesus' inward attitude or outward reactions. He does not even attribute to Jesus the relatively insignificant activities of 'going' or 'standing' or 'turning': always the expression is 'they took Him', 'they led Him', 'they dressed Him'.

As we have said, there are just nine verbs in this section of Mark's Gospel of which Jesus is the subject. One is the verb which reports His dying. Four are negative in form or meaning: 'He was silent', 'He answered nothing', 'He still answered nothing' and, when they offered Him wine mingled with myrrh, 'He did not take it'. The other four are verbs of

20

speaking. So it is literally true that, from the time when Jesus is handed over to the time of His death, He appears in Mark's Gospel to *do* nothing whatever. As to His speaking, it is markedly different from the manner of His speaking in the earlier part of the Gospel. In the earlier part of the Gospel Jesus speaks authoritatively, effectively, decisively, changing situations by His words, taking fishermen from their nets, casting out demons, stilling a storm, confounding critics, raising the dead. But after He has been handed over the emphasis falls on the fact that, for the most part, He does *not* speak: and, when He does speak, His words are always disregarded or ineffective or inconsequential or misunderstood. The first time He speaks is to protest against the manner of His arrest—'with swords and staves', as if He were a thief—but the protest ends in apparent resignation—'but the Scriptures must be fulfilled'—and it is entirely disregarded by those who are making the arrest. He speaks again in answer to the High Priest's question, 'Art Thou the Christ, the Son of the Blessed?' 'I am,' Jesus replies, 'and ye shall see the Son of Man sitting at the right hand of power and coming with the clouds of heaven.' Although these words challenge our ears they have no such effect on those who originally hear them, for they are taken as mere confirmation of what the opponents of Jesus are already asserting and as justification for what they are already determined to do. In a superficial sense these words of Jesus might better not have been spoken. The third occasion on which Jesus speaks is in answer to Pilate's question, 'Art Thou the King of the Jews?' Here His words—'Thou sayest'—are so inconsequential that they might almost be translated 'if you like', 'have it your way'. And on the fourth occasion that Jesus speaks, raising His cry from the Cross, 'My God, My God, why hast Thou forsaken Me?' His words are so misunderstood that they are taken to be a call for Elijah and evoke the irrelevant response of a sponge raised to His lips. From the moment when Jesus is handed over such words as He speaks might as well not have been spoken—they are indecisive of, and irrelevant to, the actual course and development of events.

21

So at the moment of the handing over of Jesus there is a striking change in the manner in which Mark presents his story. From this point onwards Jesus is, in a grammatical sense, the subject of just nine verbs, whereas He is the object, direct or indirect, of fifty-six; and, even when He is grammatically the subject, His 'action' is either negative or indecisive. Now, of course, any person under arrest is inevitably restrained, to some extent, from the more obvious and physical forms of activity. What is remarkable in Mark's account is that, from the critical moment onwards, he altogether ceases to ascribe to Jesus the interior activities of thinking and feeling of which, in the earlier part of the Gospel, he has written so freely; and he also ceases to mention those relatively slight but vivid touches of activity, 'walking', 'standing', 'turning', 'looking', of which the earlier part has been so full. Both these forms of 'activity' are no less possible to a person under arrest than to a person at liberty—indeed, one would expect that the interior activity of a person under arrest and threat of death would be peculiarly intense, and Mark's silence about them must be explained not simply by the change in Jesus' situation but also, and primarily, by a change in the writer's perspective. Once Jesus is handed over, Mark sees Him, consciously or unconsciously, in a different way. Jesus is still seen as the focus and centre of the story, but now His centrality is not that of the subject of activity and the initiator of events. It is that of the object of activity, of the one by whom actions are received, of the one upon whom events bear. Jesus is still in the centre of the stage, but as He stands there, silent and motionless, other characters emerge from the wings to carry the action forward; and it is upon the figure in the centre that the action of others bears. It is in this rôle—as the object of activity, the bearer and recipient of events—that Mark now sees and presents Jesus; and therefore it is not relevant to his purpose to speak of continuing activity on Jesus' part—not even if that activity consists of being brave, or reacting patiently, or forgiving. It is scarcely possible that Mark, or any Christian writer of the first century, would have thought that these qualities were absent from Jesus during the hours of His trial and crucifixion; but they pass unmentioned by Mark because his attention is now focussed upon Jesus as the object of activity, as the one who, no longer doing, is now done to. This is how Mark sees the change effected by the handing over of Jesus: Jesus is no longer the one who does—He becomes the one who is done to.

The change is indicated to the reader by a change in the writer's perspective; and this change in perspective generates a discernible change in his style and manner of writing—in the shape and syntax of his sentences. Consciously or unconsciously, Mark writes of Jesus in a different way after He has been handed over: he writes of Him as the object rather than the subject of what is happening. When we turn to John's Gospel we observe that here also the handing over of Jesus is presented as His transition from the role of doing to that of being done to, from the status of subject to that of object; but in John's Gospel the transition is not brought out, as in Mark's, by a change in the writer's perspective and style. In John's account of the trial and crucifixion of Jesus, the central figure continues, in a grammatical and syntactical sense, to be active, to *do*: He *speaks* effectively to Peter in the Garden and during His trial; He not only *responds* at some length to Pilate's questions with disturbing effect but Himself *puts questions* to Pilate; He *comes forth* wearing the crown of thorns and the purple robe, and He *goes forth* to Calvary carrying His own Cross; on the Cross He *sees* His mother and His friend and *speaks* to them with effect; He *knows* that all things are completed; He *calls for* a drink and *receives* that which is offered to Him; and finally He *says*, 'It is completed'. The transition of Jesus from subject to object is not implicit in John's Gospel in a change in the writer's perspective and style: it is brought out explicitly but subtly by the use in the later part of the Gospel of certain words, and the presentation of certain incidents, which imply the reversal of the situation which has existed in the early part of the Gospel. When John describes the handing over of Jesus and what followed upon it, He makes use of certain words and phrases which have a powerful

23

resonance for the attentive reader of the earlier part of the story and suggest to him that the role or status of Jesus is the very antithesis of that which has been presented in the earlier part.

In the earlier part of John's Gospel, from the third to the seventeenth chapters, there is much emphasis on the 'work' or 'works' of Jesus and the 'works' of the Father done by, or manifested in, Jesus. One might be inclined to think that references to the words (*erga*) of Jesus and to Jesus as working (*ergazomai*) are distributed fairly evenly throughout the Gospels, but this is not in fact the case. Matthew writes once of the 'works of Christ', and Luke once refers to Jesus as 'a prophet mighty in word and work'. Otherwise neither the noun nor the verb is used in connection with Jesus in the first three Gospels. But between the third and the seventeenth chapters of John's Gospel there are twenty-four occasions on which the words 'work' or 'working' refer to Jesus. Quite explicitly and emphatically, therefore, at this stage of the story John presents Jesus as working, as intensely active, in the name of the Father and in obedience to His will.

It is also made explicit in John's Gospel that Jesus' time for 'working' is limited. In His encounter with the blind man whom He healed on the Sabbath, Jesus says that the reason for the man's blindness is that 'the works of God may be manifested in him'; and then He continues, 'We must work the works of Him that sent me while it is day: the night is coming when no one can work.' Jesus is explaining that He must 'work' even on the Sabbath because His time for working—the 'daylight' period—is limited. Within that period Jesus must do all His work because 'daylight' is to be followed by the 'night' which, for Jesus as for mankind in general, must mean the end of work. There is the same implication, the same contrast between the 'day' with its opportunity for work and the coming 'night' when work must end, in Jesus' words to His disciples when He is proposing to go to Judaea for the sake of Lazarus. The disciples attempt to dissuade Him with the reminder that the people of Judaea recently tried to stone Him, and Jesus' reassurance is given to them in these words: 'Are there not twelve hours in the day? If a man walks in the day he does not stumble because he sees the light of this world: but if a man walks in the night he stumbles because the light is not in him.' The words are relevant to the situation and reassuring to the disciples only to the extent that the general truth which they assert applies to Jesus Himself: only if He is saying that the twelve hours of the 'day'—the time of His own 'working'—have not yet run their course. And if He is saying this, He is also saying that, in due course, His 'night' will fall—the time when He may no longer 'walk safely', the time when He may no longer 'work'.

So the period for 'working' is limited; but John makes it clear that, while that period lasts, Jesus is not only commissioned and sent to do the Father's works: He is also *free* to do them. During the daylight period His freedom to work cannot be fettered or restrained. In the early part of John's Gospel there are many references to the attempts of Jesus' opponents to restrain or inhibit Him; but always these attempts are vain. Twice they attempt to stone Him, but without effect. No less than six times are there references to the attempts or intentions or failures of His opponents or their agents to 'take' Him; but always 'no one laid hands on Him' or 'He passed out of their hands'. Ordinary people of Jerusalem are represented as surprised that one whom 'they are seeking to kill' is still able to speak 'freely'; and in the last reference to the principal opponents of Jesus during the daylight period we hear them saying to one another, 'you are doing no good: see, the whole world has gone after Him'.

John emphasizes more than the other Evangelists the opposition which Jesus met from the earliest period of His ministry; but he emphasizes yet more strongly the total ineffectiveness of this opposition. He shows Jesus working in unfettered freedom, and leaves us a picture of the many hands that would restrain Him clawing and snatching at Him in vain. He represents Jesus as claiming and exercising by the Father's will *exousia—exousia* to judge, *exousia* over all flesh, *exousia* to lay down His life and to take it again; and

25

this word *exousia* combines the ideas of opportunity, freedom and power. It is 'control of the situation', 'power of initiative', 'power of effective action'. Throughout the daylight period John shows Jesus free to work, in accordance with the Father's will, beyond the restraint or interference of human hands, even of those hands which, at one point, would have 'taken Him and made Him King'. And so, having used the daylight period to the full and without restraint, Jesus is able to announce at the end of it the completion of the work which is both the Father's and His own: He says at the Last Supper, 'I have glorified Thee upon earth: I have *finished the work* which Thou gavest Me to do.' And thereafter, significantly, we hear no word more about the work of Jesus.

Now let us observe what happens, according to John's account, when Jesus is handed over. We notice first that the handing over is closely associated, or even identified, with the coming of 'night'. When Judas leaves the Last Supper to set in train the handing over of Jesus, John tells us 'that it was night'. Commentators and preachers have for long assured us that this remark by the writer is no mere aside, no mere passing detail casually introduced. They have assured us that the phrase has a strong resonance, a deep suggestiveness. This is certainly true; but *what* precisely is the resonance, *what* exactly does the phrase suggest? The conventional answer is 'evil'; the coming of night, it is said, suggests that the powers of evil are now vigorously at work. But this interpretation of John's meaning is almost certainly wrong. For throughout his writings the word which he uses to suggest the presence or power of evil is the word 'darkness' ( *skotos* or *skotia* ): it is not the word 'night' (*nux*). Similarly the word which he uses to suggest the presence or power of good is the word 'light' (*phōs*) and not the word 'day' (*hēmera*). The association of 'night' with 'evil' and 'day' with 'good' occurs occasionally in Paul but never in John. To the attentive reader of John's Gospel the phrase 'and it was night' can have only one connotation: it must mean that the 'daylight' period is over and that the time foreseen by Jesus has come—the time at which

26

'no one can work', the time at which 'working' must give place to 'waiting'.

So the deed of Judas, the handing over of Jesus, is subtly but explicitly associated by John with the end of the period in which Jesus fulfils His Father's will by doing and completing His Father's work. It is also associated, in a most striking way, with the end of Jesus' freedom from restraint by human hands. In Luke's Gospel there is no mention of any physical 'binding' of Jesus in the course of His arrest and trial; and in the Gospels of Matthew and Mark Jesus is bound only when the Jewish authorities have examined Him and found Him, to their own satisfaction, guilty of blasphemy. But in John's Gospel, at the moment when Jesus is arrested in the Garden, He is bound there and then. The hands which previously had clawed and grasped at Him in vain are, at this moment, in a most physical and literal sense laid upon Him; and any careful reader becomes aware of a dramatic change in the situation. Jesus' unfettered freedom is suddenly changed for bondage, His impalpability to human hands for the literal and physical hold of those hands upon Him. At the moment when Jesus is handed over He passes, according to John, from unfettered freedom to total constraint.

So the handing over of Jesus is directly associated by John with the coming of 'night' and the 'binding' of Jesus—that is to say, with the transition from working to waiting and from freedom to constraint. Later in the story, when Jesus is already handed over, there are two further incidents in which the use of a particular word draws attention to this transition or reversal of the situation and points to the sharp antithesis between what is happening now and what happened in the earlier phase—the 'daylight' phase—of Jesus' life. When Jesus stands before Pilate, one of the questions put to him by Pilate is, 'Do you not know that I have *exousia* to crucify you and *exousia* to release you?'; and Jesus' reply is 'You would have no *exousia* at all over me if it had not been given you from above.' The ambiguity of the phrase 'from above' need not concern us: the striking point of the incident is that Jesus, who in the earlier phase has claimed and exercised *exousia*

27

to judge, *exousia* over all flesh, now recognizes that He is standing at the judgement seat under the *exousia* of Pilate. Once, in the 'daylight' phase, Jesus claimed and exercised *exousia* : now Pilate claims and exercises *exousia* over Him. Once Jesus was the subject of the exercise of *exousia*: now He is the object. That same change in the rôle or status of Jesus which Mark brings out by his style and manner of writing is suggested by John through a reversal in the application of a particular word. When the reader hears Jesus speak at the judgement-seat of Pilate's *exousia* over Him, he cannot but recall that once it was Jesus who possessed *exousia* to judge.

There is a similar effect on the attentive reader when he comes to that moment in the story of the crucifixion when a moist sponge is raised to the lips of Jesus. All the Evangelists record the incident, but only in John is it recorded as following upon Jesus' words 'I thirst'. These particular words carry the reader's mind to other occasions in John's Gospel when Jesus has spoken of 'thirsting': 'he who believes on me shall never thirst', 'he who drinks the water that I give shall never thirst' and, especially, 'if anyone thirsts, let him come to me and drink'. Once Jesus offered and promised to assuage the thirst of others: now He needs and seeks the assuaging of His own thirst, and those who come to Him come not to drink but to raise a drink to the lips of Jesus. The situation is reversed: Jesus appears now as the object of that activity—the assuaging of thirst—of which, in the earlier phase, He had claimed to be, and had been, the subject.

So, according to John's account, when Jesus is handed over, the 'day' which gives freedom and opportunity to work is succeeded by the 'night' when there can be no more work and by the 'binding' which takes away freedom and places Jesus in the hitherto ineffective hands of others. Now He who has previously exercised *exousia* and the power to judge passes into the *exousia* of others and stands under their power of judgement; and now He who has previously promised and dispensed the water of life to others becomes the recipient of their refreshment. In a different way, by the mention of small

28

but significant details and the use of brief but resonant phrases, John is telling us what Mark tells us: that the handing over of Jesus was His transition from working to waiting upon and receiving the works of others, from the status and rôle of subject to that of object, from 'doing' to 'being done to'.

In other words, both Mark and John identify the handing over of Jesus with His transition from action to passion, or His entry into passion. But the word 'passion' must be properly understood. We normally equate the passion of Jesus with His 'suffering'; and at an earlier phase in the development of our language that equation was probably not misleading. For in that phase the word 'to suffer' meant hardly more than 'to have something happen to one', 'to be the one to whom something happens' or, perhaps, 'to let something happen to one'. The use of the word 'suffer' did not imply, at an earlier stage in the development of our language, that what happened to one was painful or distressing or tragic. When the seventeenth-century translators of the Bible wrote, of the woman who came to Jesus seeking healing for an 'issue of blood', that she had 'suffered many things of many physicians', they did not imply—in the ears of their contemporaries—that the treatment which the woman had received had been painful or her physicians brutal; and when they wrote, of Pilate's wife, that she had 'suffered many things in a dream' on account of Jesus, their words would not necessarily have suggested to their contemporaries that the dream had been a distressing or terrifying nightmare. In the seventeenth century, 'to suffer many things' meant simply 'to have a great deal happen to one'; and what is being said by the seventeenth-century translators as they turn the original Greek into the language of their day is simply that the sick woman had had a great deal of treatment and that Pilate's wife had had a long or vivid dream about Jesus.

But to the ears of the man of today the word 'suffer' has an immediate and inevitable connotation of pain or distress or loss. The translators of the New English Bible recognize this; and in both the passages mentioned they have made no use

29

of the word. They have recognized that the verb 'to suffer' is no longer an appropriate translation of the Greek verb *paschō* which appears in the two passages.

Now it is from this verb *paschō* that the English word 'passion' is ultimately derived. Strictly speaking, the verb *paschō* is simply the converse of *poiō*: *poiō* means 'to do', *paschō* 'to be done to'. If we combine each of these verbs with the adverb *eu*, meaning 'well', we get the phrases *eu poiō*, meaning 'I treat somebody well', and *eu paschō*, meaning 'I am well treated'. To translate the latter as 'to suffer well' would at the present time be completely misleading: for it would suggest not that I am well treated but that I bear pain or loss with courage and patience. *Paschō* is not, in the modern sense of the word, 'to suffer': it is 'to be done to', 'to be affected', 'to have something happen to one'. In the opening sentence of Plato's Apology, Socrates pays a wry compliment to his accusers who have just completed the case for the prosecution: 'I do not know', he says to the jury, 'what happened to you as you listened to my accusers, but they spoke so convincingly that I for my part almost forgot who I am.' The phrase 'what happened to you' is a translation of the verb *paschō*—of that verb used in a characteristic way. Socrates does not know—or affects not to know—whether the jury found his accusers' case convincing or unconvincing, pleasant or unpleasant to listen to: whether they were delighted or offended, gratified or outraged by what they heard. But all these possibilities—the possibilities of being affected in all kinds of different ways—are included by the use of the verb *paschō*. The verb does not refer *to the manner in which* the jurors were affected by what they heard: it simply implies that they were affected *in some way or other*.

Whenever it is possible, words should be used with respect for their etymological roots. When we speak of the passion of Jesus we should be referring not to His suffering, not to the pains which He endured or the cruel manner in which He was treated by the hands of men, but simply to the fact that He was exposed to those hands, affected by whatever those hands might do. With this understanding of the word 'pas-

30

sion', we may say that the moment when Jesus was refreshed by a moist sponge was as truly a part of His passion as the moment when He was scourged or the moment when His hands were nailed to the cross; and, conversely, we must deny the contention of some preachers that, because the earlier life of Jesus contained elements of hardship and distress, we may think of His passion as 'lasting all through His life'. The distress and weariness of work and the hardships of travel are not, as such, 'passion'. To be faithful to the Gospel record we must reserve the expression 'the passion of Jesus' for that distinct phase of His life into which He entered when He was handed over to wait upon and receive the decisions and deeds of men, to become an object in their hands. What happens in both Mark and John when Jesus is handed over is not that He passes from success to failure, from gain to loss or from pleasure to pain: it is that He passes from doing to receiving what others do, from working to waiting, from the role of subject to that of object and, in the proper sense of the phrase, from action to passion.

We perceive, then, how the Gospel writers 'see' the handing over of Jesus—what it actually means to them. In our first chapter we discerned that the fact that Jesus was handed over was of great importance to the Gospel writers—a fact to which, by the prominence given to the deed of Judas and the manner in which that deed is described, they constantly draw the reader's attention. Now we perceive, as it were, the interior nature or quality of the fact: we perceive what the fact is that the Gospel writers felt to be of such great importance. The fact is that, at a certain point in His life, Jesus passed from action to passion, from the rôle of subject to that of object and from working in freedom to waiting upon what others decided and receiving what others did. The Gospel writers seem to reflect the conviction of the earliest Christian believers that, whatever else was said about Jesus, it *must* be said that He was handed over; and they show, as they tell the story, that what they understand by the handing over of Jesus is His transition from the free activity of a subject to the passion or receptivity of an object.

31

Here then is something which both the archetypal Evangelists, Mark and John—each in his own way—are telling their readers very emphatically about Jesus. Both of them, deliberately or instinctively, present a figure who, at a certain point, exchanged action for passion, the role of subject for that of object. A theologian who accepts the argument and evidence which we have set out may be inclined to pass immediately to such questions as, 'Why, in the mind of the writers, did this exchange come about?' 'Why, in the purpose of God, may it have come about?': 'What implications do the Evangelists themselves see in it?' 'What implications should we see in it?' For a theologian these are entirely proper questions. But the ordinary reader who has got so far may be more inclined to ask, 'What has all this to do with me?' 'What connection is there between the "fine print" of the story of Jesus and the problems and questions which arise in my own life?' This demand for 'connections' seems no less proper in its own way than the technical and systematic questioning which comes to the mind of the theologian: indeed the reader who demands connections is perhaps already showing himself, in a certain sense, a theologian. Partly for his sake, and partly to give a fair account of the actual sequence of our own thoughts, we shall at this point turn aside from the picture of Jesus in the Gospels to consider an aspect or area of contemporary life with which that picture seems to connect—an area of life (or, in fact, a number of areas) in which we ourselves make that kind of transition which the Evangelists discern and emphasize in the life of Jesus. We shall notice that at the present time we tend to find this transition both inevitable and difficult—difficult to accept, difficult to come to terms with—and we shall argue that the root of the difficulty may lie, at least in part, in the manner in which we see Jesus or, more exactly, in the manner in which we see the God Who, according to the Christian faith, is disclosed and presented to us in Jesus. Having thus discerned a connection between our image and understanding of Jesus and the commonplace yet pressing difficulties of our own lives, we shall return to the 'fine print' of the Gospels, hoping to discern what further depths of meaning may be present in the handing over of Jesus—in that transition from action to passion which is of central importance in the picture which two at least of the Gospel writers present of Him.

# 3

# The Status of Patient

To a person who, in the prime of life, is suddenly struck down by a serious accident or by a debilitating illness—a stroke, a perforated ulcer or a coronary thrombosis—there often comes a particular moment when he recognizes his helplessness. His first reaction after being involved in a road accident may be to climb out of his car or get up from the ground; and, when the sudden pain of illness grips him, he may at first attempt to conceal or ignore it and to 'struggle on'. But often, at a certain moment, the struggle shows itself to be unavailing and impossible to sustain, and at this moment the patient 'gives in'. He simply remains in his car or on the ground and waits for help; or he retires to bed and asks his wife to call the doctor; or he grasps the telephone and requests an ambulance.

Thereupon his place and status in the world undergo a sudden and remarkable change. Up to this point he was ordering and arranging his own affairs and, very probably, the affairs of a number of other people also. He was holding the reins of a team of projects and purposes—major and minor, public and private; he was taking action, initiating policy, making decisions—some of which affected people other than himself. At the least he was creating his own immediate future and was in control of his own immediate destiny. But now, suddenly, he passes into the hands of others and becomes dependent on their decisions and actions. He is lifted by the crew of an ambulance, transported to hospital, examined by doctors, monitored by machines, eased by injections, sustained by intravenous drip, reassured by nurses, visited by

34

friends. What happens in the next few hours and days happens *to* him, is done *to* him; and the satisfactoriness or unsatisfactoriness of a particular day depends hardly at all on himself or his own efforts and decisions. A 'good' day is one on which a machine or instrument shows a certain reading, or a drug has a certain effect, or solid food is allowed, or a doctor expresses himself pleased with the progress, or a particular visitor comes: and conversely with a 'bad' day. The sick or injured person has now become a *patient*; and it is relevant to our present reflections to note that the word 'patient' takes its origin, via the Latin, from that Greek verb πάσχω with which we have previously been concerned. A person who becomes a patient enters into passion; he becomes one who is done to, is treated; he becomes the object of the decisions and care and treatment of others. He becomes aware of the dependence of his own destiny upon what is decided and done by others; and this is no doubt the reason why most patients become unwontedly sensitive—sensitive to a degree that surprises even themselves—to what is said and done by the people in whose hands they are. A person who in normal life is relatively self-sufficient, relatively indifferent to the opinions, attitudes and remarks of others, often finds himself, when he becomes a patient in hospital, extraordinarily pleased or affronted by the passing remark of a nurse, a porter or the boy who brings the papers.

The victim of a serious road accident or of certain kinds of illness passes suddenly, in a matter of seconds, into the condition and status of patient. The transition is dramatic and unmistakeable. Many other people make the same transition gradually and by imperceptible stages—through advancing years, increasing infirmity and slowly changing circumstances. Many people enter, step by step, into a phase or condition of life in which, although they may not actually be called patients, they depend, for the satisfactoriness or unsatisfactoriness of life, hardly at all on their own actions and decisions and almost entirely on what is done to and for them by others. Towards the end of our life-span some degree of dependence on others is normal and expected: we accept the likelihood, and even the inevitability, that the very last phase of our life will be a 'second childhood' in which we shall be no less dependent on the care and attention of others than we were in our infancy. So it has always been. But in the world of today there seem to be certain factors which not only prolong our final phase of dependence but also extend and introduce the condition of dependence into earlier phases of our life. In the world of today the status or condition of patient is not confined to passing periods of illness and a brief phase of final infirmity: it seems to be experienced in ever new areas of life and to occupy an ever-increasing proportion of life. The condition of the patient upon the hospital bed— examined and monitored, prescribed for and provided for, sustained physically and emotionally by external agencies— appears to be ever more typical of the condition of man-in-general, or at least of man in the developed Western world. The transition which is made dramatically and suddenly by the victim of an accident or a coronary thrombosis is being made gradually and imperceptibly by Western man in general: the status of patient is becoming ever more widespread and familiar in our world.

Let us examine this matter in some detail. It is obvious in the first place that the development of medical skill and social care has extended the normal life-span in the Western world. Such skill and care keep us alive for a longer period: perhaps they keep us active and energetic for a longer period. But the very phrases which we naturally use—'they keep us alive', 'they keep us active'—suggest the manner in which medical skill and social care present themselves to us. They are not our own resources: they are external aid and support on which we depend. So they present themselves to our consciousness; and, in practical terms, ever-increasing numbers of people find themselves, in a literal sense, constantly waiting upon medical attention and social service. In districts where a high proportion of the population is elderly a great deal of commonplace conversation and commonplace anxiety is centred upon the quality of such attention and service in the district; for this quality is felt to be a major constituent of the general quality of life. So for an increasing number of people the possibility of a 'good life' depends to a considerable degree on the possibility of receiving adequate medical and social support, on the possibility of being watched over and attended to in a diligent and reassuring way. In the kind of district to which we are referring any change in the structures of local care and support—the retirement of a well-known doctor, a change in the procedures of the social services, the re-siting of a surgery or clinic—arouses widespread anxiety. It raises a question—not the question 'What shall we do about it?' but the question 'What will become of us?' It may well be true that the characteristic anxiety of our age is not the anxiety of the young about what they should make of their lives but the anxiety of the elderly about what will become of them. Certainly the question 'What will become of us?' is often heard among elderly people; and it vividly reflects the speaker's awareness that the satisfactoriness of his life at this stage must depend not so much on what he achieves as on what he receives, not so much on what he himself does as on what is done to and for him.

Clearly, then, the development of medical and social care must increase the number of people for whom a satisfactory life is primarily and necessarily dependent on the provision of external support and attention. Similar effects seem to follow from the increasing practice of early retirement—whether voluntary or compulsory. The most distinctive fact about a retired person is that he is no longer achieving, by his daily work and his weekly or monthly pay, the wherewithal to live. The pension, or the income from savings, on which he now lives has in all probability been earned in the past; but it is not being earned by his present activity. Now his income, and all that is made possible by his income, is received by him, and the receipt of it no longer depends on any kind of effort or activity on his part. A retired person may be active in many ways; but his activity is no longer self-supporting, self-sustaining. No longer is a retired person achieving, day by day and week by week, a roof over his head, food on the table, the necessities and luxuries which constitute his standard of living. These things are provided; and any variation in their provision depends not at all on his own diligence or achievement but on such external factors as government policy, the rate of inflation and the state of the stock market. So with retirement there often comes a profound change of consciousness. One may continue to be active in many ways, but it is no longer possible to regard one's activity with entire seriousness. For it is no longer upon what one does that one's basic well-being depends: it is upon what is provided for one by the government, the pension-fund or the stockbroker. So it is generally expected, both by and of retired people, that in what they continue to do they will 'fit in with', and give priority to, the life-supporting and therefore more 'important' activities of their younger associates. At one time people now retired were the parents of young children; and then the children waited for the attention and availability of their busy parents. But now, in retirement, these same parents find themselves waiting for the attention and availability of the grown-up and busy sons and daughters. At one time these parents arranged treats and excursions for their young children; but now, in retirement, they find such arrangements made for them by their adult sons and daughters. Retired people usually find that their life now contains a larger proportion of waiting—waiting upon the availability and convenience and arrangements of other people. A good day, a good Christmas or a good holiday depends less than once it did upon their own initiative and activity and more upon what is done and arranged by other people. By the simple fact of retiring—at whatever age and in whatever state of health—and so coming to receive financial provision, a retired person tends to find himself 'provided for' in other ways also: he finds his life more dependent than once it was on the availability and organization of other people.

As retirement comes earlier, an increasing proportion of people become dependent, for the satisfactoriness and richness of their lives, on what is done to them and for them. A similar consequence will follow if, as seems probable, a high level of unemployment becomes normal and inevitable in industrialized countries. At the present time unemployment brings with it a relatively low level of income, so that to be unemployed is, almost always, to be poor. This conjunction of unemployment with poverty is obviously not inevitable; for it is possible to imagine a society so well equipped with mechanical and electronic aids that the level of production rises rather than declines with the loss of 'jobs', and it is also possible to imagine that in such a society the fruits of production might be so distributed that provision during unemployment was scarcely less than average earnings from work. In such a society the unemployed would no longer be poor. The fact remains, however, that they would still be provided for. Like retired people today, they would still be receiving rather than achieving the wherewithal to live; and it is likely that the same kind of psychological and social consequences would appear. A society in which unemployment exists will always be 'two nations': even if the distinction between rich and poor is overcome by a more equal distribution of the fruits of production, the distinction will remain between those who are providing for themselves and those who are provided for, between those who achieve the wherewithal to live and those who receive it. It seems that, for the foreseeable future, a large and probably increasing number of people are likely to fall into the second category, living a life of that kind of economic dependence which tends also to generate psychological and social dependence.

We have pointed to certain expanding areas of life—old age, retirement, unemployment—in which the quality of a person's life becomes largely dependent on factors external to him, factors which are neither achieved nor controlled by his own effort and initiative. Such a person becomes, in the sense in which we have used the word, 'a patient'. And in the modern world the status of patient can be discerned not only in what may be considered untypical conditions—old age, retirement, unemployment—but also at the heart of normal working life.

What does 'normal working life' mean for the majority of people in modern industrial society? It does not mean a private and individual performance of which the outcome depends primarily on one's personal qualities of strength, tenacity, skill or ingenuity; and 'a good day at work' does not mean a day on which one has used such qualities fully and effectively. To 'work' is, for many people, to be 'a cog in the wheel'; or, to put the matter less tendentiously, to be at one's place within a system and to perform the task which is appropriate to that place. Whether or not that task is, and can be, properly performed depends far less on one's own personal qualities than on the proper operation of other parts of the system—on the provision to one, at one's place, of the necessary input of power and information. A 'good day at work' is, on the whole, a day on which there are few 'problems'; and the problems in question are not, for the most part, one's own lack of strength or skill or diligence. They are the interruption or failure of the necessary provision of power or information—the failure of the electricity supply, delays in the post or on the telephone, the breakdown of a machine, the absence of a blueprint from the office or a decision by a higher authority. The individual operator is both contributor to and dependent upon the system as a whole; but since other parts of the system make themselves noticed by him principally when their failure obstructs his own operation, he tends to be more aware of his dependence upon the system as a whole than of his contribution to it. The system presents itself as that upon which his own operation depends, as that upon which he himself must wait if he is to perform his own task. In ever-widening areas of modern working life the individual operator finds that his own possibility of achievement, success or satisfaction depends almost entirely on the efficient functioning of a system over which he himself has no control. In this sense he tends to feel himself the patient, the object and even the victim of the complex system within which he works; and this feeling seems to be largely justified.

Not only at work, but also in private life, in home life and leisure, the man of today increasingly finds himself the recipient rather than the achiever of what is satisfactory or unsatisfactory. It has often been pointed out that modern forms of entertainment (and the word itself is significant) are increasingly 'passive' rather than 'participatory'; and the point is often made critically, to demonstrate the idleness or degeneracy of people today, especially those of the younger generation. The criticism is probably unjust. When Johnson and Boswell made their celebrated Tour of the Hebrides, their motive, as Boswell puts it, was 'reasonable curiosity . . . to contemplate a system of life almost totally different from what we had been accustomed to see'; and it may well be the same kind of 'reasonable curiosity' that draws a person of today to contemplate the various and remarkable images which appear on the television screen. His motive may be not at all inferior to that of Johnson and Boswell: the difference between his case and theirs is simply that what he 'contemplates' will depend not at all on his own initiative or activity. His 'reasonable curiosity' will be satisfied only to the extent that is permitted by the programme: he has no possibility, as Johnson and Boswell had, of discovering what lies beyond the headland which appears on the screen or of penetrating to the inside of a croft of which he is shown the outside. He may learn as much in his armchair as they on their laborious travels; but the limit of what he can learn is set not by his tenacity as a traveller but by what is presented to, or provided for, him.

The mention of travel suggests another area of life in which, in recent years, activity has given away to passivity. At one time travel was a notable exercise of human initiative and endurance: to make a journey was an enterprise demanding skill and character, and to arrive on time at one's destination was a triumphant achievement. Even so recently as the early days of motoring drivers would gather in their overnight lodging to discuss with some pride the techniques of gear-change and acceleration by which they had negotiated the steep hills of Devon or Derbyshire, the skill with a map by which they had found their way through the lanes of Warwickshire and the ingenuity with which they had put right one or more of the frequent, but usually remediable, malfunctions of the cars of that period. But the driver of today is in a quite different situation. The successful completion of his journey depends hardly at all on the human accomplishments which filled his predecessors with pride. It depends almost entirely on such external factors as the state of the traffic, the extent of roadworks on the motorways and, in the event of a breakdown, the availability and proximity of professional help. Much the same is true of other forms of travel—so that we speak nowadays not of *making* a journey but of *having* a journey, and proverbial wisdom about the enterprise of travel—'travel broadens the mind', 'to travel hopefully is better than to arrive', 'he travels fastest who travels alone'— is quite inapplicable to the experience of the air traveller, the commuter or the motorway driver. It is well said that modern man no longer travels: he is transported.

So in ever-increasing areas and phases of his life the man of today finds himself exposed to factors beyond his power to influence or control, and knows the quality of his life to be largely dependent on such factors. This conclusion seems to be in direct contradiction of the cliché that modern man has achieved a mastery of his environment beyond the wildest dreams of his ancestors. But the cliché is true only if one means, by 'man', the human race as a whole and, by 'his environment', the natural environment of earth and water and plants and animals. If one means, by 'man', the individual, and if one includes, within the term 'his environment', the complex technical and organizational system within which he lives, then it is clear that man is less than ever master. A primitive man, trapped between a rising river and a wood inhabited by dangerous animals, would still have certain possibilities of action by which to overcome his predicament. At least he might suppose himself to have such possibilities, and might resort hopefully to the propitiation of the river-god or vigorously to the use of his digging-tool. But a man of today, trapped by an electricity failure in the heart of a modern city, has, and knows himself to have, scarcely any possibility of effective action. He must simply wait until power is eventually restored by some distant and unseen agency—an agency at least as far beyond his influence and control as the powers of nature and the gods were beyond the influence and control of his primitive ancestor. The complex 'environment' of modern man—an environment which includes everything from cables hidden in the ground to information stored in computers and from his own credit-rating to the fluctuations of the money-market—certainly does not present itself to the individual as an instrument or servant of which he is the master: often it presents itself as a capricious overlord of which he is, at best, the beneficiary and, at worst, the victim.

We must not, of course, exaggerate the dependence of modern man upon factors and agencies over which he has no control. Obviously there remain in his life enclaves and even wide areas in which he exercises large and unfettered freedom, in which there is scope for individual enterprise and achievement, and in which the quality of a man's life lies largely in his own hands. The point is that these areas are tending to diminish, and that the preservation of such as remain requires ever more determined and self-conscious vigilance. Deliberate efforts to survive 'outside the system', to create and maintain a life-style of independence, self-sufficiency and personal responsibility, are a relatively new phenomenon in the developed world; but they suggest a gallant protest against 'the way things are going' rather than a significant reversal of it. By and large our view of the foreseeable future must be of a world in which the individual lives ever more and more in the condition of 'patient', dependent for his general well-being on complex factors beyond his influence or control, receiving rather than achieving whatever quality his life possesses.

Now the important fact is that our conscious and explicit attitudes to this condition are almost wholly negative. In practice we largely acquiesce in our condition: either there seems to be no alternative, or the alternative involves a degree of heroism or eccentricity which most of us find unacceptable. But in theory, in conscious reflection and discussion, we regret, resent or repudiate our condition. In our public stance, so to speak, we either deplore or deny our private status. Although we acquiesce in practice in our condition of dependence we see no positive worth or value in it; and where it is possible to assert or pretend to independence, so we do and so we are expected to do. In our public attitudes we locate the value of life exclusively in those areas where, actually or allegedly, we are free from external dependence and are exercising our own initiative and creating our own achievement.

This public attitude is so widespread that it appears in the most commonplace incidents and conversations. We compliment and congratulate very elderly people on being 'still so active', 'still so independent'. The form or result of their activity, the manner in which they use their independence, is so secondary a consideration that it is usually ignored: that they are active and independent is, *per se*, good and admirable. And elderly people themselves find it necessary, or at least appropriate, to deplore those aspects of life in which they are dependent on other people, and to emphasize and exaggerate those in which 'they manage for themselves'. There is between many elderly people and their younger associates a tacit and affectionate understanding that much shall be made of what the elderly do for themselves, and that whatever help is needed shall be given unobtrusively and even furtively. It is felt necessary to a satisfactory old age that an elderly person should be assured, whether truly or falsely, that he is 'useful' to himself and others, that his services are 'needed', that he is 'contributing' to the general well-being. That he is being helped, supported and cared for is a matter for which—possibly—he should be grateful; but it is a matter which should not be brought home too forcibly lest it should damage or impair his 'self-respect'. It is conventional wisdom that the pension or benefit received in old age should never be represented as 'assistance' but always as that to which the recipient is 'entitled', as that which he has earned or acquired by right.

The attitude which is felt necessary to the preservation of self-respect among the elderly is felt equally necessary in relation to those who are handicapped or disabled at an earlier stage of life. The emphasis in agencies of social care is now on 'enablement' rather than 'help'; and the change of

44

terminology is significant even when no change is involved in the procedure and practice of the agency. 'Enablement' focusses attention on what the disabled person can, or will be able, to do for himself. It draws attention away from the 'provision' of, let us say, an artificial leg and towards the possibility of the recipient's 'getting around on his own'. The presupposition behind the new terminology is, of course, that what a person does for himself, as his own achievement, is of higher worth than that which is done to or for him by the help of others: that the practice of independence is, in itself, of greater worth or dignity than the condition of dependence. The enablement of an artificial leg does not necessarily mean that a disabled man will get out more and go to more interesting places than he did when his wife pushed him in a wheelchair, nor does it necessarily mean that his wife will be glad to be relieved of a back-breaking chore. For it is not unknown for a dependent person to receive from his active partner a 'provision' richer than anything that he could achieve by his own independence and for the active partner to find delight and satisfaction in making that provision. Nevertheless, the enablement which leads to independence is considered to be always appropriate; and a man would be thought lacking in self-respect if, after receiving the enablement of an artificial leg, he continued, for his own pleasure and his wife's satisfaction, to be pushed around by her in a wheelchair. The disabled person—or the hospital patient— who is so content to receive that he fails to do for himself everything that he can do is generally considered to be either inadequate or selfish or lacking in self-respect. To accord to another person the status of patient—of one who must be helped—is generally considered offensive; and to accord that status to oneself is generally considered demeaning.

The terminological change involved in speaking of 'enablement' rather than 'help' is, as we have suggested, significant in itself. But frequently there goes along with it an actual change of policy—a concentration of research and resources on those human conditions in which the patient may be 'enabled' in the direction of independence and a corresponding neglect of those in which the patient requires permanent 'help'. A victim of paraplegia is often acutely aware of the change of conditions if and when he is moved in hospital from the ward where such patients are trained in mobility and self-help to the ward allocated to those who do not respond to training and must depend permanently on the help of the staff. He is likely to notice that the staff of the second ward are less numerous and less fully trained than that of the first; and he will almost certainly notice that, whereas the first ward contained a good deal of new equipment specially designed for his enablement, the equipment that is available in the second ward to the staff who help him—by feeding him, lifting him in and out of bed and attending to his bodily needs—has scarcely changed in the generation since his father was a patient there. Such a patient may well feel that his removal to the second ward has been a relegation: that since he has failed to achieve relative independence he has become less worthy of society's attention and expense: that now that he is assessed as wholly dependent his condition is less well esteemed than when he was potentially independent. The policy of enablement, for all its valuable consequences, seems also to carry with it the unfortunate implication—or at least suggestion—that those who are beyond enablement are worthy of only a lesser degree of attention and expense.

There are other areas of life in which our professed and public attitudes suggest a certain distaste or contempt for the status of patient, the condition of dependence. In retirement, for instance, many people feel obliged to represent themselves as 'busier than ever'. As we have noticed, retirement often brings with it a larger element of what might be called 'social waiting'—of waiting upon the arrangements and convenience of younger associates who are working; but this degree of dependence, though it may be acceptable in private, is not easy to admit in public. Few retired people are able to admit that they are 'just passengers nowadays': and if the admission is made it will usually be contradicted, briskly if affectionately, by younger members of the family. Our public attitude is that retirement should be filled with all kinds of new activi-

46

ties—with 'creative leisure'; and that, unless a retired person is engaged in this way, he will be—or at any rate will feel—diminished. So we feel it right to encourage our retired parents to engage in new 'interests' or 'hobbies', or at least to represent them as so engaged; and most retired people feel it right, at least in the way they represent themselves, to conform to what is expected for them.

This public understanding of what retirement should be, though perhaps disturbing to those who are inwardly content to sit back and rest and wait upon the world, is relatively harmless—partly because retired people, with the experience of life behind them, feel the pressure of public opinion less keenly than the young. More serious is the public attitude which is often displayed towards that other condition in which one is 'no longer working'—the condition of unemployment. Unemployment is often described publicly as a 'degrading' condition. Now it is, of course, undeniable that, at the present time, to be unemployed is to be relatively poor, and that many people who are unemployed find themselves bored and dissatisfied; and the condition of anyone who is both poor and dissatisfied is a condition which a humane society will want and try to rectify. But the description of unemployment as a degrading condition suggests more than this. It suggests that, however well an unemployed person may be provided for and whatever he himself may feel about his condition, that condition is, objectively, of less worth and dignity than that of a person who is working and thereby earning the wherewithal to live: and the unemployed person who finds his condition difficult enough on account of the poverty which, at the present time, accompanies it must find it yet more difficult to bear when he hears from politicians that it is in itself an indignity or a degradation.

But the contention that unemployment is degrading is not, of course, simply a political ploy: it seems to reflect a very widespread assumption that a person who, in the prime of life, is receiving rather than achieving his livelihood is, by that very fact, diminished in dignity—even if what he receives is adequate to his needs and even if he is quite content to be

47

receiving it. If the assumption is valid, if it is in fact a degradation for a person capable of working and earning to receive rather than achieve his livelihood, then the society of the future in which the increase of automation and the development of robot-technology is likely to diminish the availability of human 'jobs', must inevitably be a society full of shame and degradation. But our immediate purpose is neither to question nor to assent to the contention that unemployment is, in itself, degrading: it is simply to point out that the contention is widely expressed and that it presupposes that the condition of the person who depends upon and receives from others is, *ipso facto*, of less dignity and worth than that of the person who works and achieves for himself.

Let us note finally our professed and public attitudes to our dependence on 'the system'—on the complex structure of inter-related operations which constitutes the environment of both work and leisure for an ever-increasing number of people. The system is designed for smooth and efficient operation. It is gradually built up and modified in order to facilitate each of the many operations of which it consists—in order to make power immediately available, at the flick of a switch, to the operator of a lathe; in order to make information instantly available, at the press of a button, to the decision-maker or administrator. Unless for the most part the system has this facilitating effect it will collapse or cease to be used or be replaced. Of course defects in the system will from time to time obstruct individual operations: and so involvement in and dependence upon a complex system both facilitates and obstructs. But if, on balance, facilitation does not outweigh obstruction a system is unlikely to survive. On the face of it, therefore, our world of ever more highly developed and complex systems should be a world of ever-increasing facilitation for the individual: and so, in an objective sense, it undoubtedly is. The point scarcely needs labouring; but it might be illustrated by the recent and successful achievement of the American Space Shuttle. This technological triumph was made possible by a complex system through which experts in various disciplines could draw widely on, and be facilitated by, the research and resources of experts in parallel or subordinate disciplines—in which, one might say, a great pyramid of mutual facilitation was erected with the creation of the Shuttle as its apex and goal. The system worked and the goal was triumphantly achieved—achieved as it never could have been achieved by a single individual or by many individuals working in isolation. But it is extremely significant that subsequent reports of the operation of the system indicate that the experience of those who were engaged in it was, primarily, not of facilitation but of *frustration*—the frustration of constantly waiting upon, or being held up for, the outcome of the research of other specialists and the information provided by them. The waiting was, in general, fruitful and rewarding in its outcome. Nevertheless, despite its fruitfulness and triumphant outcome, it was described, even in retrospect, by those who waited as constant frustration.

Now this would suggest that 'frustration'—an experience reported so frequently in the modern world that the word has become part of our most common coin—is caused not so much by the occasional failure of systems as by the constant necessity of waiting upon them. One is frustrated not because the system constantly fails to deliver but because one must constantly wait for it to deliver—because one has no alternative to waiting, no personal action or initiative to which one can resort in lieu of that which the system, in its own time, delivers. Frustration begins in awareness of oneself as waiting of necessity on factors beyond one's control, as dependent on those factors; and it is very evident that, in general, this awareness gives rise to dissatisfaction, anger and resentment. The word 'frustration' describes not merely our awareness of dependence but also our resentment of it; and the increasing frequency with which the word is heard indicates how widely and generally such resentment is felt. Objectively we value the facilities and services which modern systems provide—from the supply of light and heat to the delivery of the mail; but we do not easily accept the necessity of receiving them on, as it were, their own terms, the fact of being dependent on them or 'ruled by' them. Whenever, through the necessity and experience of waiting, our dependence 'comes home to us', it seems improper and offensive and generates tension, anger and resentment. Then, very frequently, we speak of our frustration and, in doing so, we disclose our assumption that the waiting rôle, the condition of dependence, the status of patient, is improper to us, a diminution of our true function or status in the world, an affront to our human dignity.

We have argued in this chapter that, on the one hand, the social and economic organization of the Western world is developing in such a way that, in ever-increasing areas and phases of life, the individual is cast in the rôle of patient, of recipient rather than achiever, of one who must wait and depend upon factors outside his control. We have argued, on the other hand, that this rôle is, on the whole, resented. Whenever possible, this rôle is repudiated, denied or concealed; and when it must be accepted and recognized it gives rise to frustration and a sense of affronted dignity or diminished worth. Public opinion accords the highest worth and respect to those individual and corporate enterprises which are intended to maintain and enlarge the areas of human independence, to increase the possibilities of personal achievement, to provide greater scope for private initiative, to 'enable' people into self-reliance and self-sufficiency. But perhaps these enterprises are no more than gallant or despairing gestures, no more effective than sand thrown against the wind or Mrs Partington's broom wielded against the advancing ocean. Perhaps the transition of the individual into a condition of ever more marked dependence or receptivity or passion is, for the foreseeable future, irreversible.

This possibility must be taken seriously: the way the wind is blowing must be recognized. But realism about the shape of the future need not necessarily lead to pessimism or depression. For the professed and public attitudes of today do not necessarily express the final truth about human worth and dignity or about the proper rôle and status of man in the world. It is not necessarily the case that man is most fully human when he is achiever rather than receiver, active rather than passive, subject rather than object of what is happening.

50

It is possible that public attitudes are based on an improper or at least questionable assumption—an assumption that will not stand up to scrutiny. In the next chapter, therefore, we shall look more closely at this assumption and consider what grounds there may be, in history or experience, in ethics or theology, for the widespread contemporary belief that when a man is the object rather than the subject of what is happening in the world he becomes, to that extent, diminished in human stature, deprived of human dignity.

# 4

# The Roots of Impatience

In his Life of Johnson, Boswell tells of an occasion when Johnson diverted himself by attempting to *shock* the company of high-born ladies and gentlemen among whom he was sitting. He raised his voice and addressed Sir Joshua Reynolds. 'Pray, Sir Joshua,' he said, 'how much do you think that you and I could earn in a week if we both worked as hard as we could?'

In our day it is not intended as a shock to the audience when a man of aristocratic birth or inherited wealth explains and illustrates on the television how hard he works. Rather the reverse. In the eyes of a contemporary audience it will be a credit to such a man that he works and, by working, goes some way to earning his privilege and wealth. That a man, any man, should in some way work, earn and achieve is thought, in our age, an essential qualification if he is to retain the respect of his contemporaries and his own self-respect.

Evidently it was not so in the age in which Johnson lived and the circle in which he moved. In his earlier years Johnson had worked with a diligence, a tenacity and a 'drudgery' which still impresses us today; and thereby he had won his fame and achieved his acceptance among some of the aristocracy. But evidently it was 'shocking' to draw attention to this fact. 'Politeness' required the fiction that Johnson was where he was by birth or breeding, by superiority of taste or other natural endowment—by almost anything except his own hard work and earning and achievement. And the social values which require this kind of fiction have been accepted in circles far outside the aristocracy of eighteenth-century England.

The Greek gentleman for whose benefit and instruction Aristotle wrote his ethical treatises did not aspire, and was not expected, to earn or achieve his place in the world; nor did the courtier at Versailles or the heroine of Victorian fiction. Among such people 'style' rather than achievement was the criterion of worth and the ground of mutual esteem; and the style of the leisured classes to which they belonged often involved an ostentatious dependence on the attention and assistance of a multitude of slaves or personal servants. Admittedly this dependence was, to a degree, an affectation: a Greek gentleman was not physically incapable of so 'banausic' a task as preparing his own food, nor were all the courtiers of Versailles incapacitated by their girth from putting on their own clothes. It was not by reason of the master's incapacity but by reason of his will and command that the slave or servant attended him. Nevertheless dependence on others was considered appropriate, if only as an affectation; and often, no doubt, it was by no means an affectation. No doubt there were many among these leisured classes who were so well schooled in the style of dependence and had cultivated it so long that they were in truth widely incompetent and had no alternative but to rely on the attention and assistance of slaves or servants. Fiction, in fact, from the Roman comedy to the Victorian novel, is full of such instances—of situations, comic or tragic, in which the life of a master or mistress has become totally ruled by the purposes or whims of servants.

Vestiges remain to this day of the attitudes and affectations so widely accepted in earlier phases of society. There is a type of man who 'makes a point'—and it is a point of 'honour' rather than a mark of selfishness—of 'knowing nothing' of such 'menial' tasks as cooking a meal or decorating the house or repairing the car, and of relying for the performance of such tasks on someone else; and there is still, even in this age of women's liberation, a type of woman who feels that her proper function in the world is to be 'looked after' or 'treasured' or even 'spoilt'. Furthermore, the idea is by no means extinct that the importance of an administrator or executive and of his particular work is to be measured and assessed by the number of those who 'service' him in it; and it is not uncommon for such a person to repair damage to his self-esteem by adding to his staff.

Such vestiges of earlier attitudes are no doubt unimportant in themselves. They may survive as private eccentricities but they are no longer professed or advocated as public policies. But their survival may remind us that the professed and public attitudes of today are by no means 'rooted in human nature', are by no means the only attitudes and assumptions through which society can be preserved and the individual retain his self-respect. In large areas of society, over long periods of time, many people have felt no psychological necessity to achieve, no moral obligation to work or earn or contribute: many people have been content to receive and acquiesce in that place in the world which was ensured by birth or breeding, by inheritance or education: many people have felt it not alien to their self-respect but necessary to it that they should adopt or affect a life-style of total dependence on the attention and service of others. So it is that many people have thought and lived in the past, and so it is, no doubt, that, in some less 'developed' societies, many people think and live today.

We may deplore such attitudes and assumptions and attribute them to a primitive or outdated scale of values. But clearly we cannot say that only *our* public attitudes are 'rooted in human nature', or that it is more 'natural' to man to find his satisfaction and self-respect in work and achievement than to find it in inherited distinction and the receipt of service. The most cursory glance at earlier phases of society establishes that it is no more 'natural' to admire a person for having earned and achieved his present affluence than to despise him for having done so, and no more natural to resent one's dependence on others than to cultivate and even flaunt it.

So one can easily refute, by even the briefest glance at history, any suggestion that only the public attitudes of to-day—those attitudes which locate the worth and dignity of man in his exercise of initiative and independence, in his

54

activity and achievement—do justice to the basic instincts and drives and needs of human nature. And these attitudes are also questionable from another point of view. They seem more acceptable in theory than in practice, more viable as counsels for public policy than as counsels for private behaviour. They are the attitudes which we feel it right to profess and embody in public policy but not the attitudes which we are moved to adopt under the immediate pressure of those concrete situations in which we are personally involved. In many situations the total dependence of a person on others, his or her total helplessness, seems to give to that person a unique, remarkable and undeniable importance. Now the word 'importance' is admittedly vague; but we can give to it a little more precision by pointing out the *catalytic* effect of the presence of a helpless person, the effect of his presence in changing a situation and giving rise to a variety of new possibilities. Nothing so disrupts the normal and expected procedure of a meeting as the physical collapse of someone who is present: nothing so decisively interrupts a game as an injury to one of the players. The presence of a helpless person suddenly generates in such a situation a whole new range of possibilities—the positive response of attention or the negative response of indifference, the application of good sense or the display of panic, effective action or ostentatious emotion, skill or clumsiness in providing help, hesitation or impetuosity. The helpless person becomes the stimulus of a variety of reactions and responses, the catalyst of a range of distinctive deposits. In his presence, as a result of his helplessness, a great many things happen which would not otherwise happen—things which both display and affect the characters and dispositions of those around him. It is in this sense that the helpless person becomes, in his helplessness, extremely important. The back-bencher who collapses at a meeting becomes at that moment a focus of attention and a stimulus to action as he never was when he was making his ineffective speeches.

Let us consider two illustrations of the extraordinary importance of a person who is almost totally dependent on the attention and help of others. In an area of new housing, to which people had come from many different localities, there were many complaints about the absence of the 'neighbourliness' and 'feeling of community' which had been familiar in the older districts; and several agencies—the Tenants' Association, the Churches and the social workers—were engaged in well-meant but rather ineffectual efforts to 'create a community'. But in a certain small area of the district, amounting to some fifteen or twenty houses, it was evident that a sense of community already existed. Here neighbours were to be seen talking in the gardens or going into one another's houses: people knew their neighbours' names and where they came from: garden equipment was shared and borrowed: mothers took neighbours' children to the shops. A stranger would soon have detected the reason for this unusual state of affairs. At the centre of the small area lived a woman, the mother of five children, who was confined strictly to bed for several months with severely ulcerated legs; and the common decency of those who lived nearby would not allow them to ignore the helpless predicament of this mother. They attended to her and her family. In so doing they came to know one another and, in an informal way, to work together in sharing out the necessary tasks; and so the much desired 'neighbourliness' of the older districts was soon created. Now it was not, in this case, the charm or gratitude or any other personal quality of the helpless woman which created community around her; for she was in fact more resentful at 'having to depend on others' than appreciative of what those others did, and was full of complaints that 'life was passing her by'. It was her sheer helplessness, her resented and resentful helplessness, which was having a social effect which important agencies were trying in vain to achieve; and in a period when, allegedly, 'life was passing her by', she was, in a sense, a more 'important', a more 'valuable', person than at any other period of her life. At that period she might well have been called a 'public benefactor'—not through any qualities of character which she displayed in her helplessness but through the sheer fact of her helplessness.

A second and more poignant illustration of the extraordinary importance of a dependent and helpless person is to be seen in those families where one of the children is severely handicapped, physically or mentally. All parents, of course, would wish such a child to become 'enabled' and competent and increasingly independent; but sometimes this is a dream rather than a possibility. In such cases many parents will, in moments of confidence, speak movingly of the 'enrichment' or 'blessing' which the helpless child has brought or been to themselves and the whole family. It is a truism that those for whom 'most has to be done' tend to be the most dearly loved; and it is understandable that the power of helplessness to kindle and attract love may deepen and enrich the whole texture of relationships within a family. So a child who has no power of action or initiative and scarcely any power of response may become the focus not only of the family's attention but also of its profound gratitude. It is also true, of course, that there are some few parents, and perhaps a slightly larger number of brothers and sisters, who would admit, in moments of frankness, that the presence of a handicapped child had created disruptive resentments or debilitating restraints within the family, and that the texture of life in the home had been strained or impoverished. But whether for good or ill, whether the outcome be triumph or tragedy, the presence of a permanently helpless member within the family circle probably has deeper effects on the life of that circle than the presence of any other member; the child who can 'do nothing' for himself or anyone else often becomes the pivot upon which the happiness or unhappiness of the whole family turns.

In such circumstances a person who can be no more than the patient or object of other people's activity is seen to be extremely important. The consequences of his existence are incalculable: his presence makes a profound difference to the way the world is in that place. It might be argued, however, that this 'importance', though undeniable, is not the importance which is appropriate to a human being, that it falls short of the importance which is proper to man and upon which his human dignity depends. It might be argued that *things* no less than people can be important as objects: that an ancient building which is in need of preservation may be no less a stimulus to the creation of community than a bedfast woman who is in need of help: and that some treasured possession of a family—the family home or the family dog—may, on occasion, be no less the pivot of family happiness than a handicapped and helpless child. The importance of man as object, it might be said, is only a secondary importance, shared by many things and creatures in the world: the unique and exclusive importance of man, that which gives to him his uniquely human status and dignity, is his importance as subject—as source and initiator of activity, as creator and achiever. So, it might be argued, the importance of man as object falls short of fully human importance: *that* is present only in the exercise of his capacity to be a subject.

Let us consider this argument. Man is certainly endowed with a remarkable capacity for initiative, action and achievement. But so are many other creatures. Many creatures are remarkable for the vigour and precision of their activity and for the beauty or utility of their achievement. All living creatures are active: we even speak of some inanimate phenomena of nature—volcanoes, atmospheric depressions and sunspots—as 'active'. The uniqueness of man clearly does not lie simply in his capacity for action—for that is shared by many other creatures and things. It must lie rather in the variety and flexibility of his capacity for action. It is the manifold and seemingly endless diversity of man's capacity for action that makes him remarkable among the creatures of the world and can reasonably be held to justify his claim to a unique status and dignity.

But if the uniqueness of man as subject lies in the fact that his potential activity has so many facets, it is pertinent to notice that man as object is also a creature of many facets; that man has a manifold and various capacity not only to act and achieve but also to be done to, to be affected, to receive. To put the matter grammatically, a human being may be the object of almost as rich a range and variety of verbs as that

58

of which he may be the subject. An inanimate object—a stone in the street—may be the object of only a limited range of activities, a limited number of verbs. It may be looked at, weighed and measured, transported in various ways, heated or cooled, broken up. A living creature, especially a domesticated creature, may be the object of a rather longer list of verbs: in addition to what may be done to a stone it may be fed or starved, restrained or released, trained in certain ways, hurt, killed. But when we consider the verbs of which a human being may be the object the list becomes very long indeed. In addition to what may be done to a thing or a domestic animal a human being may be questioned, refuted, criticized, embarrassed, inspired, amused, humiliated, flattered, betrayed, enlightened, patronized, corrupted, acquitted, invited, appointed, honoured, excused, argued with, appealed to—and so on and so on. A human being might be likened to a radio receiver capable of picking up a very wide range of frequencies—a receiver, moreover, which can be so finely tuned as to differentiate between signals received on immediately adjacent frequencies. That is to say that a human being—at least a mature human being—is capable of being the object not only of a wide range of verbs—from, let us say, 'to torture' at one extreme to 'to inspire' at the other—but also of varieties of verbs which are distinguished one from another in meaning only in the most fine and subtle way. One may perhaps 'praise' a dog; but only with reference to a man would one ask whether, in being praised, he is in fact being 'flattered' or 'patronized' or 'encouraged' or 'admired' or even, if the praise is faint, 'damned'. A large part of human maturity seems to consist in the ability to identify precisely what it is being done to one by and through the actions of others—to distinguish 'being admired' from 'being flattered' and 'being corrected' from 'being rejected'. A person who receives all praise as admiration and all reproof as rejection is an immature person.

Among the many and various activities of which man can be the object, there are a large number of which *only* he can be the object: only a man can be inspired, obeyed, questioned, refuted and so on. For a castaway on a desert island with no human companions many activities would be impossible through the absence of a human object; and of the many activities of which he would be deprived some would belong among the most esteemed and respected of human activities. The castaway would not be able to inspire or educate or welcome or console or respect; he would not be able, in a fully human sense, to serve or love. To the possibility of some of the most esteemed of human activities the presence of a human object is no less necessary than that of a human subject; and if there were fewer facets to man's capacity to be the object of activity there would be fewer also to his capacity to be the active and achieving subject. Very often in everyday experience we encounter people whose aspirations to 'care' or 'teach' or 'serve'—or, less admirably, to 'command' or 'dominate'—are totally frustrated by the absence of anyone who is available and willing to be the object of such activities. The frustration of such people—the 'emptiness' which they experience in their lives—is evidence enough of the importance of man in his rôle as the object or recipient of the activities of others.

Man's capacity to be the object might be called his 'passibility'; and the point of our argument is that the variety of man's potential passibility seems no less remarkable than the variety of his potential activity. It seems unreasonable therefore that the unique status and dignity of man in the world should be thought to depend simply on his rich and manifold potential for activity. Human dignity seems—to put it crudely—'to have another leg to stand on' in the manifold and various passibility of man. Human passibility as much surpasses, in its manifold and minute variety, the passibility of things and living creatures as human activity surpasses in its variety and flexibility the activity of natural phenomena and insects and animals; and if the first gives to man a unique status and dignity in the world, so also does the second. When Shylock claims that a Jew has no less right to revenge than a Christian, no less worth or dignity or right to justice, he bases his claim not on the similar achievements or activities of Jews and Christians but on their shared and common passibility. 'Is not a Jew', he asks, 'fed with the same food, hurt with the same weapons, subject to the same diseases, healed by the same means, warmed and cooled by the same summer and winter as a Christian is?'

We have noticed the importance of the person wholly dependent on others—of a woman strictly confined to bed, of a helplessly handicapped child. We see now that this importance does not fall short of fully human importance. When a person becomes an object he is no more reduced to the level of a thing or animal than when, being a subject, he performs some activity which a thing or animal can also perform. In each case alike man is raised above the condition of thing or animal by his manifold potential—whether for activity or for passibility, whether for doing or for being done to. 'To treat people as things' is to be blind to, or forgetful of, the *many facets* of their passibility.

The question therefore arises, 'Why is it that, in the professed and public attitudes of today, the proper function of man is identified exclusively with the exercise of his capacity for action, and that his human dignity is alleged to be preserved only to the extent that he acts, initiates and achieves?' We have already noticed that certain societies of the past have accepted quite different criteria of man's proper function and quite different canons of human dignity; so it cannot be said that only the public attitudes of today are 'rooted in human nature' or that only they can point the way to the satisfaction of basic human instincts. We have also argued that the public attitudes of today do less than justice to the remarkable fact of the richness and variety of human passibility. It begins to appear therefore that the presuppositions which underlie contemporary attitudes are questionable and even arbitrary, and that their roots may lie not in the fundamental nature of man but in the shallower soil of the historical, social and economic facts and changes which have shaped that particular area of society which we call the Western world.

To put the matter briefly, the Western world has become

what it is through the exploitation of man's capacity for production. We use the word 'exploitation' in no particularly derogatory sense; for it is obvious that the generality of people in the Western world have been beneficiaries no less than victims of the system which has organized their lives and labour to increase their capacity for production. The point is simply that, from its earliest stages until recent times, the capitalist system has needed and used the masses of mankind primarily for their labour, for their capacity as producers. It may well be that at present, as production is increasingly achieved by self-regulating machinery, men are required by the system rather as consumers than as producers. But the fact remains that for several centuries the economic function required of most men in the Western world has been that of producer, of worker. It is as producers and workers that most men have been important and necessary to the system; and it would be strange indeed if a man's economic function in a system so powerful, so revolutionary in its effects, did not have profound effects on his understanding of his total function in the world—his personal, social and even his religious function. A man whose failure to produce brings economic disaster to himself and his family is not likely to escape the conclusion that it will bring social, moral and spiritual disaster also; and in the upbringing of his children he will implant this conviction in them from their earliest years. He will teach them, as moral and religious principles, that they must be useful, that they must be busy, that Satan always finds a task for idle hands to do; and, if they should jib at the burden of unremitting toil that is laid upon them, he is likely to explain, not simply that this is required of them for economic survival, but that it is inherent in the condition of fallen humanity or prescribed by the purposes of God. Productive work, required of most men during the phase of expanding capitalism, seemed vindicated in worth and value by the triumphant achievements of the system; and general acceptance of the superiority of a man's productivity over every other aspect of his being both invited, and was sustained by, a religious interpretation of man's calling in the world as, primarily, a calling to produce, to contribute, to work. Useful and productive work was seen, in the period of expanding capitalism, not only as an economic necessity but also as a moral duty and a religious calling: it not only sustained man's existence in economic or material terms but also 'justified' his existence in moral and religious terms.

But it would be naive to suggest that what is normally called the Protestant work ethic was simply improvised or invented in order to support the demands of the system for an ever-increasing work force or to provide religious justification for the life of grinding labour which was often required of men. No doubt the needs of the system encouraged the acceptance of the ethic; but they did not necessarily originate or produce the ethic. It is far more probable that the needs of the new system, and the opportunities which it presented, brought into the forefront of men's minds certain ethical principles which were already implicit in the religious inheritance of medieval Europe—principles, that is to say, which can be detected at a deep and fundamental level in the deposit of Christian doctrine which was the inheritance of the Middle Ages.

We are suggesting then that, in the first place, the public attitudes of the present have their roots in the quite recent past: that our tendency to identify the unique dignity of man with his manifold capacity to work and achieve has much to do with the need of an expanding capitalist system for a multitude of human producers. It may well be that our economic system has now passed into a phase in which men are needed rather as consumers than as producers; but ethical principles which were implanted in the earlier phase persist as the presuppositions of new phase. And we are also suggesting, in the second place, that the work-ethic which dominated in the phase of expanding capitalism and persists today may be sustained, as it were, by a tap-root which reaches down to early periods of Christian history and fundamental levels of Christian doctrine.

We detect this tap-root in two ancient and continuing themes of Christian belief and teaching: the first that man is made 'in the image of God', the second that God Himself is *actus purus* or 'pure activity'.

It has been a persistent theme of Christian teaching that, of all that God has created, only man is created in His image. It is this that gives to man his unique status in the world and invests his being with unique worth. Of course it is recognized that the image of God in man is defaced or marred—that man does not in fact mirror in his own face the face of God. But that he should do so remains his proper goal and function, the purpose of his being. Within the limits of creatureliness man is to resemble God—a possibility given to no other creature. So man retains his unique status and dignity in the world to the extent that he does resemble God: and to the extent that he fails to resemble God he fails to retain his proper status and loses his human dignity and becomes degraded.

So man's understanding of what God is determines his understanding of what is proper to his own status and dignity; and in the formative period of Christian thought it was established, or appeared to be established, that, in terms of that contrast between action and passion with which we are concerned, God is pure activity: that He is always subject and never object: that He is 'impassible'. The philosophical background out of which this conclusion emerged, and the reasoning which seemed to justify it, do not concern us at present. It is enough to note that the doctrine of the impassibility of God became formally accepted in the Christian tradition; and like all matters of doctrine, however technical or abstruse they may appear, it has had in the long run, through preaching and popularization, profound effects on the understanding and imagination of the ordinary believer. In the popular imagination God is He Who initiates, originates, acts and gives: Who is wholly self-dependent: Who controls all situations: Who exercises unfettered freedom in performing His works and achieving His purposes. The activity which the popular imagination discerns in God is often, admittedly, a very slight and effortless activity: it is, as it were, by the merest gesture of His hand that He creates a world or determines the destiny of a nation. But the point is that, beyond this effortless activity, the popular imagination discerns *nothing* in God: no dependence, no waiting, no exposure, nothing of passion or passibility, nothing of the status of patient. And therefore, when these conditions appear in the life of man they must appear fundamentally 'ungodlike'; and therefore again they must appear alien to the proper status of man and unworthy of his unique dignity. They may be attributed to the merely creaturely aspect of man's being—to that aspect in which he is merely 'one of the primates'—or to the *marring* of the image of God in him—to the fact that he is 'fallen' or sinful: they cannot be attributed to that image itself or be seen to belong to man's unique and proper condition as bearer of that image. Man will be seen to 'live up to' the divine image which he bears only to the extent that he acts, initiates and achieves—only to the extent that his place in the world is a place of work.

It would of course be absurd to attribute the professed and public attitudes of today—the attitudes of politicians, social workers, medical practitioners and the man in the street—directly to the apprehension and acceptance of traditional Christian doctrines. It is not of the nature of God nor of the image of God in man that most social workers are thinking when they speak of 'enabling' rather than 'helping', nor most elderly people when they show how active and independent they are, nor most wealthy peers when they explain to the public how hard they work. The immediate roots of such attitudes in such people go down, no doubt, simply to their own childhood when their parents trained them, as they themselves had been trained, to be busy and active and useful and, in due time, independent. We are still not far removed in time from the period when this kind of training was essential to the health of the economic system and to the economic survival of the individual. But although the direct roots of the attitudes in question may be of comparatively recent formation, we are suggesting that they are sustained or supplemented by a tap-root which grows from a deep level within the religious tradition of the Western world. The politician who speaks of man's 'right to work' or his 'need for a satisfying job' is not likely to be consciously grounding his argument on Christian principles, and it is still less likely that he will have before him a clear and explicit vision of God and of the image of God in man. But, unless he is speaking purely by rote, he must have in mind some kind of criteria of what is needful to man and owed or appropriate to man; and it is not likely that these criteria will be wholly unconnected with the religious traditions of the society to which he belongs. To put the matter no higher, the politician who so speaks will not feel that he is opposing the principles of religion but will rather expect that those who take their stand on these principles will be whole-heartedly on his side.

This expectation of the politician is justified. The long-taught Christian doctrines of the image of God in man and of the impassibility of God do seem to imply, when taken together, that the role in the world which is uniquely appropriate to man is the role of active subject, of initiator, creator and achiever; and that in the opposite role of patient, of recipient, of dependent object man falls below his proper stature and status and dignity. Now, as we have argued, this latter role seems to be becoming ever more widespread and familiar and inescapable; and we see no likelihood of a reversal of this trend or tendency in the developed world. For the foreseeable future the individual is likely to find himself, in almost every aspect of his life, increasingly dependent on a complex system of organization and technology, and increasingly limited in his possibilities of private initiative and personal achievement. Either this dependence and limitation must be a source of increasing resentment and frustration and even self-contempt; or there must be a rediscovery of the dignity which belongs to man as patient, as object, as one who waits upon the world and receives that which is done to him. We have suggested, by drawing attention to the remarkable range and variety of human passibility, a line of thought which might assist this rediscovery; but progress seems to be impeded by the continuing influence of the Christian tradition with its conjunction of belief in the impassibility of God with belief that the dignity of man consists in his conformity to the image of God. The impediment would be removed if we could simply abandon the Christian tradition and persuade others to do so; but, for ourselves, we find this unacceptable and even impossible. The alternative is to look more closely at one or both of those elements of Christian belief which, taken together, constitute the impediment.

It is at the doctrine of the impassibility of God that we shall look; and we shall do so by returning to the conclusions which emerged from the first two chapters of this book and attempting to work forward from them. The purpose of this and the preceding chapter has been to suggest that the attempt is worth making—to show that the conclusions of the earlier chapters are of no mere historical or narrowly theological interest but are highly relevant to the recovery of man's sense of dignity and worth in those increasing areas of life in which he finds himself dependent on others, exposed to factors beyond his control, waiting upon events, the object and recipient of what happens around him and is done to him.

We end this chapter with a vignette which may perhaps disclose the heart of the problem with which we are wrestling. A bishop of the Church, a man of long and great achievement, became towards the end of his life totally blind and so much afflicted with a number of different illnesses and disabilities that he was confined to bed and almost deprived of the power of movement. He lay supine on the bed, his arms limp, the palms of his hands upwards, so that his very posture suggested his total exposure to whatever might be done to him, his total dependence and helplessness. As one stood beside him on a particular morning some weeks before his death, one had a sudden and overwhelming impression that something of extraordinary significance was going on before one's eyes—something that even surpassed in its significance all that the bishop had done in his years of activity and achievement and service. This impression did not arise from the manner in which the patient reacted to his condition—from any obvious evidences of his cheerfulness or courage: for he

67

spoke hardly at all, and there could be no other expression of his thoughts or feelings. The impression seemed to come, strangely, from the totality of his helplessness and exposure. He was now simply an object exposed to the world around him, receiving whatever the world might do to him; yet in his passion he seemed by no means diminished in human dignity but rather, if that were possible, enlarged.

In the years of activity and achievement the bishop was rightly known as a godly man, as one in whom the image of God is less marred than in most of the sons of men. Was that image obliterated in him, or effaced, or distorted when he entered his final phase of passion? Did he now less bear the likeness of God than when he worked and achieved? The memory of him and the indelible impression which one received at his bedside makes it impossible to answer these questions in the affirmative, and gives added urgency to our task of discovering how it can be that man may bear, in passion no less than in action, the image of that impassible God of whom Christianity has for so long spoken.

# 5

# The Road to Gethsemane

When a Christian believer is going through any distressing or disquieting experience, it can be a source of comfort and encouragement to him to remember that the Lord Jesus 'knows all about it'—that He Himself went through the very same experience. So when such a person is severely tempted he may be helped by the remembrance that Jesus also was tempted; and when he is let down or deserted by friends he may be consoled by the thought that this same thing happened to Jesus. It is especially in the experience of acute physical pain that believers—and perhaps some who are not formally believers—find strength and courage in the thought that Jesus went through the same experience—in the thought of the nails and thorns and the pain that He must have experienced on the cross. History tells of Joan of Arc strengthened in the flames by the cross of plaited straw held before her eyes; and memory records a young man dying of cancer who, in the half-hour of agony when each injection of morphine was losing its effect, would slowly move his right hand across his body and cling to the Palm Cross tucked in his pyjama pocket. That Jesus went through pain is a continuing source of comfort and courage to pain-stricken people.

One might, when one is free from pain, raise questions about the logic of such comfort—about why it is that pain should be more bearable or more bravely borne for the knowledge that Jesus—or indeed anyone else—has borne similar pain. But questions of logic do not arise for a person in acute pain: it is enough that he should find it good and strengthening to turn his thoughts to Jesus in His pain or to rest his eyes or fingers on a representation of the cross.

So it may be that the thought of the handing over of Jesus—of His transition from action to passion—can be of practical help to people who must face, or have already faced, a similar transition in their own lives. We have already stressed that the word 'passion' does not mean, exclusively or even primarily, 'pain': it means dependence, exposure, waiting, being no longer in control of one's own situation, being the object of what is done. So the passion of Jesus 'connects' not simply or even primarily with the human experience of pain: it connects with every experience of passing, suddenly or gradually, into a more dependent phase or area of life—with going into hospital, with retiring or losing one's job or having to wait upon the actions of other people and other factors beyond one's control. If the thought of the passion of Jesus is helpful at all, then it may be helpful not only to the person who is bearing the 'cross' of pain but also to the person who feels that he is 'on the sidelines', that he has become useless or ineffective, that he is no longer making his mark in the world or his contribution to it. 'To be handed over' in ways such as these is particularly disquieting to a person who, by habit or temperament, has been exceptionally active and energetic or a notable achiever; and such a person may well find comfort in the thought that a similar pattern appears in the life of Jesus—that He also passed from activity and work and achievement into a final phase of waiting and dependence and passion.

So the 'fine print' of the story of Jesus with which we were concerned in the first two chapters of this book does have a connection—at least for the devout believer—with some of those difficulties and frustrations of modern life which were the theme of the two following chapters. It is *immediately* relevant to some of the personal problems of today that Jesus was handed over. But this immediate relevance is an emotional relevance—a help perhaps to the devout believer but of questionable value for the generality of people. Most people who regard their own transition to passion as a sad misfortune—as sheer diminution or even degradation—will be inclined to view the passion of Jesus in the same way. They will see it as a 'sad end' to the life of Jesus that He fell into the hands of the Jewish authorities and Pilate, to be treated as they chose; and therefore, even if they remember what happened to Jesus, they will still see their own tragedy as tragedy. The deep-rooted presupposition that the only function proper to man is activity will not be immediately eradicated by the knowledge that even Jesus Himself passed eventually into passion, for this *could* be regarded simply as a misfortune which Jesus shared with the majority of mankind.

The fact that Jesus passed into passion will not in itself be an adequate basis for a positive understanding and a willing acceptance of our own experience of passion. But such understanding, such acceptance, might emerge from consideration of the reason for which and in the manner in which Jesus passed into passion. It might emerge from recognizing that, according to the Gospel story, the transition which Jesus made was no mere misfortune but rather a kind of triumph, no diminution of Himself or His calling but rather a kind of elevation. If a man should be guided by the Gospels to see such worth and quality in the transition which Jesus made, then—and perhaps only then—he may have a possibility of seeing his own transition in a new and more favourable light.

So, in quest of this possibility, we must return to the fine print of the Gospels. First of all we shall notice one point which appears striking and significant in the Gospel of Mark and two similar points in the Gospel of John.

Mark's account of the passion, crucifixion and death of Jesus ends with the declaration of the Roman centurion standing near the cross, 'Truly this man was the Son of God.' Scholars have doubted whether a Roman centurion would have said such a thing and whether, if he had, he would have meant, by the phrase 'the Son of God', what a Christian means. But these doubts do not affect the relevance and significance of these words: they do not affect our understanding of what, through these words, the writer of the Gospel is telling his readers. Whether or not Mark has accurately reported what a centurion said, he has clearly offered to the reader in these words his—the writer's—own testimony. At the forefront of his Gospel Mark wrote, 'The beginning of the Gospel of Jesus Christ, the Son of God'; and now, as Jesus dies, the reader is offered, from the lips of an eye-witness of the event, the testimony, 'Truly this was the Son of God.' Now the question we must ask is this: what, according to Mark, has the eye-witness seen such as to draw from him this decisive testimony? What has the eye-witness seen Jesus display or do or achieve? What decisive words has he heard Him speak? The answer—which is already evident from our second chapter—is 'nothing at all'. According to Mark, from the time when Jesus was handed over until the moment when He died, He said nothing decisive and did nothing at all. According to Mark's account, the centurion would not and could not have seen anything remarkable in what Jesus said or did: for there was nothing such to be seen. All that he could have seen, all that there was to be seen, was what was done to Jesus: the figure before his eyes was simply done to, exposed to whatever the people around Him might say or do. There is nothing in Mark's account to suggest to the reader that the centurion has observed great heroism or patience on Jesus' part, or that he has seen portents or supernatural events which might be thought to indicate the passing of a 'god'; and the absence of all such elements in the Marcan account becomes the more striking when we observe that Matthew, by contrast, not only mentions such portentous events as an earthquake at the time of Jesus' death but also explicitly attributes the centurion's testimony to the fact that he has seen such things. We must insist that, according to Mark, the centurion saw nothing but Jesus 'being done to', and that it is from this perception that the testimony emerges that 'this was the Son of God'. According to Mark, the passion of Jesus was not His human misfortune: it was the decisive manifestation of His divinity.

A very similar understanding is present in the Gospel of John. According to John, the final word of Jesus on the cross was 'It is completed': and this final word was preceded, a moment before, by His perception that 'all things were now

72

completed'. Now the attentive reader will recall that at the Last Supper, before He was handed over to passion, Jesus announced that His work was completed. Evidently therefore something other than 'work' must be completed before 'all things' are completed and before the triumphant cry can be raised that '*it* is completed'. Something beyond 'work' is necessary to the completion of Jesus' function or mission or calling: and that other necessity can be nothing other than the phase of passion which, as Jesus raises His final cry, is now coming to its close. According to John, the passion of Jesus is not His human misfortune but the completion of His divine purpose and mission in 'coming into the world'.

A second point, more complex but of even greater significance, is to be observed in John's Gospel. In the earlier part of that Gospel there are many references to 'glory' and 'glorification'. We read of Jesus, the Son, glorifying the Father: we read of the Father glorifying the Son. Probably we are to understand that the Son, in His willing conformity to the Father's will, both receives the glory of the Father and so reflects that glory that in Him it becomes manifest and evident in the world. So there is, as it were, between the Father and the Son a mutual glorification, a mutual relationship which is an endless enhancement of the one divine glory. Now we observe in the Gospel of John that the divine glory is manifested or enhanced in Jesus in two distinct phases or at two distinguishable levels. We hear Jesus' prayer, 'Father, glorify Thy name', and the answering words, 'I *have glorified* it and *will glorify* it again'; we hear Jesus' words at the Last Supper, 'now the Son *is* (or '*has been*') *glorified* and the Father is glorified in Him. And God *will* glorify Him . . .'; and we hear Jesus say again at the Last Supper, 'I *have glorified* Thee on earth: and *now glorify* me in Thyself with the glory which I had before the world began.' Here are suggestions of two phases or dimensions of 'glorification'; and the first phase or dimension is closely connected with the performance by Jesus of the *works* of the Father. So Jesus says that the fatal illness of Lazarus has come about 'for the sake of the glory of God, in order that the Son may be glorified through it'; and when He

73

is about to call Lazarus from the tomb He promises Martha that, if she has faith, she will 'see the glory of God'. Even more explicit is Jesus' final word about His work: he says to the Father, 'I *have glorified* Thee upon earth: I *have completed the work* which Thou gavest me to do.'

So the divine glory is manifested in the works of Jesus, which are also the works of the Father. But so far is the phase of Jesus' work from being the *final* manifestation of the divine glory that John can say of Jesus that, during this phase, 'He was not yet glorified'. When Jesus is being glorified in such works as the raising of Lazarus, a further phase or dimension of His glorification still lies in the future. Where, in what events, are we to discern this further phase? It is conventional wisdom among theologians that John discerns or locates the further and ultimate dimension of Jesus' glorification not in one single event but in a continuum which includes His passion and death, His resurrection and ascension and possibly also His gift of the Spirit at Pentecost. What is seen by other writers as a sequence of four or five distinct events is seen by John, we are told, as a complex continuum—the glorification or exaltation of Jesus; and so clear and consistent is John's vision of this continuum that the raising up or exaltation of Jesus upon the cross is already invested, in the eyes of John, with that same glory which other writers discern only when He is raised up from death and exalted into heaven. With this interpretation of John's thought we do not disagree. But we may still ask whether, in John's account of the continuum which is the ultimate glorification of Jesus, there is any particular moment when the divine glory becomes powerfully evident in Jesus, so evident as to be perceived by man and to impress and overwhelm them.

There is indeed such a moment, and it is precisely the moment at which Jesus is handed over and enters into passion. Judas, the hander-over, comes to the Garden of Gethsemane with an armed band, and Jesus asks them, 'Whom do you seek?' They reply, 'Jesus of Nazareth'; and Jesus answers, according to John, in the words *egō eimi*. Now it is of course perfectly possible and correct to translate these words into

English as 'I am He', 'I am Jesus of Nazareth'. But neither John nor any reader of his Gospel who was at all familiar with the Greek translation of the Jewish Scriptures, the Septuagint, could be unaware that *egō eimi*, I AM, is also the sacred Name of God, the Name disclosed to Moses. Jesus' reply to the armed men *could* be heard and understood as the most awesome announcement or disclosure of His divinity, and it is in this way that the men *do* hear and understand it. For they draw back for a moment and fall to the ground overwhelmed.

In John's Gospel alone among the Gospels there is no Transfiguration of Jesus upon a hill-top—no moment when chosen witnesses have a brief glimpse, a brief visual perception, of Who He really is and are overwhelmed by what they perceive. In John's Gospel the Transfiguration of Jesus is, so to speak, transferred to the Garden of Gethsemane at the moment when He is handed over; and those who are overwhelmed by it, and bear witness to it by falling to the ground, are the men who have come to take Him into their hands. It is as Jesus is handed over, as He enters into passion, that the ultimate dimension of the divine glory becomes manifest in Him and evident to men.

Clearly then neither Mark nor John regards Jesus' transition to passion as His human misfortune. The phase of passion is necessary to the completion of His mission or purpose in the world: His transition to passion discloses the ultimate dimension of His divine glory, and it is one who has been eyewitness of His passion—and only of His passion—who is able to perceive and announce that He was the Son of God. These 'statements', clearly written in the fine print both of Mark's Gospel and of John's, are of great importance. If we take them seriously they clearly rule out any possibility that the handing over of Jesus was mere misfortune, or that the passion phase of His life was a phase of diminished significance—a mere coda to the phase of activity and work and achievement. To put the matter rather crudely, it would be nearer the truth to say that the passion phase was the 'greatest' phase of Jesus' life.

In an earlier chapter we wrote of the entirely negative attitude which the man of today tends to take to the areas or phases of passion which appear in his life. Here in the two archetypal Gospels we discern a quite different attitude to the phase of passion in the life of Jesus. Here the attitude is that the 'greatness' of Jesus culminates in His passion. So the question arises whether the passion of Jesus is of an entirely different order from our own experiences of passion: whether there is in it some unique quality or meaning which is absent from our own experiences of passion. If this is the case then Jesus' passion is, in an important sense, irrelevant to our own: it is a 'special case', and reflection on it will not affect or modify the negative attitude which we take to our own experience of passion. If, on the other hand, Jesus' passion bears any substantial resemblance to our own, then it is possible that, learning from the Gospels the 'greatness' of His passion, we may discern traces or fragments of that same greatness in our own, and so may be able to take a more positive attitude to the areas of passion which are present in the life of the modern world. So the question is clearly important, and we must examine it with some care.

Now undoubtedly there is within the Christian tradition a tendency to treat the passion of Jesus as a special case—as altogether *sui generis*. The tendency arises out of our inclination to see unique and special significance in the *death* of Jesus and to regard His *passion* as simply the necessary preliminary to His death. If it is believed that the death of Jesus, the physical extinction of His life upon the cross, had the unique power and effect of saving us from our sins or reconciling the world to God, and that the passion of Jesus—the handing over by Judas, the trial, the condemnation, the scourging and mockery—was simply the means by which that effective death was brought about, then the passion of Jesus seems to have very little connection with, or relevance to, our own experience of passion. It must have been *sui generis*, unique in being the necessary means to a unique end. Its greatness—if that is the appropriate word—must have lain simply in its being the means to the uniquely effective death of Jesus, and can

76

have little connection with any elements of greatness in our own experience. If the 'purpose' of the handing over of Jesus was simply that He might be put to death and that the unique effects and benefits of His death might be achieved, then there is little resemblance between the transition which appears in His life and those familiar transitions from action to passion which are so frequent and so much resented in our own lives.

Undoubtedly, as we have said, there is a strand within the Christian tradition which locates all the significance of Jesus, and all the benefits which we receive from Him, in the fact that He was put to death. From this point of view, the all-important fact about Jesus is that He was put to death; and if He had not been put to death the benefits which we receive from Him would not have been received. This view is firmly maintained by many Christians; but it must be recognized that there are many other Christians who find it difficult to accept. In the eyes of these others, who include the writer, the view in question presupposes a belief in the sacrificial power and effect of death which they cannot share. They recognize that at one time such a belief was normal and unquestioned: that it was widely believed in many societies that the putting to death of a victim—human or animal—could have uniquely powerful effects and benefits in sealing a treaty, a promise or a marriage; in solemnizing a building or an occasion; in cleansing impurity, expiating sin or pro-pitiating an affronted deity. They recognize also that the early followers of Jesus, sharing this belief, would naturally link the benefits which they knew themselves to have received from Jesus with the fact of His poignant and dramatic and early death, and would interpret that death as the unique source and origin of those benefits. It would have been strange if, in the early period of Christian reflection, such an interpretation had not been advanced and accepted; and even today almost all Christians would accept it in a metaphorical sense, as an image or simile of the truth. But to accept it as literal truth and to use its literal truth as the premise of logical deduction is as far beyond the intellectual capability of many Christians today as it would be to discuss and determine the spatial

77

location of heaven in relation to the solar system and the distant galaxies.

To such people an observation which appeared in our first chapter will be important—namely, that some of the early Christians, when seeking to articulate or interpret the meaning of Jesus, made use of the phrase 'He was handed over for us'. This phrase is by no means identical in meaning with 'He died for us' or 'He was put to death for us'. Far from it: the phrase draws attention not to the physical death of Jesus but to His entry into passion; not to the fact that He was put to death as a victim but to the fact that He was exposed as an object; not to the fact that He was killed by men but to the fact that He was treated in whatever way men chose. The phrase emphasizes the significance of the passion of Jesus rather than that of His physical death. Of course in the event the outcome of His passion was His death; but this does not imply that His passion was simply the necessary or chosen means to His death. It does not imply that Jesus' death discloses *the purpose for which* He was handed over: it may rather suggest that the death of Jesus discloses *the extent to which*, the unconditionality with which, He was handed over. If we say that Jesus was 'handed over unto death' we do not necessarily mean that He was handed over in order that He might be killed: we may mean that He was so totally, so unreservedly, handed over that the ultimate possibility that He would be killed was not excluded.

We saw in the first chapter that the deed of Judas in handing Jesus over was, in a historical sense, of no great importance. For already, by His open presence in Jerusalem at that time, Jesus was exposed to whatever His powerful opponents might do; and His presence there was brought about not by the designs of Judas but by His own will and purpose—a will and purpose in which He sought to conform to the will and purpose of God. So Paul, excluding all reference to Judas, can say that Jesus 'handed Himself over' and that God 'handed Him over'. These phrases, we must repeat, do not imply that the death of Jesus was willed by Himself or by the Father: they imply that what was so willed was His

78

passion, His unconditional exposure, His exposure 'unto death' to whatever the hands of men should do to Him.

Let us attempt, in the next few pages, to tell—in summary form—the story of Jesus in such a way that the focus of our attention and of Jesus' purpose is His passion rather than His death, His exposure 'unto death' rather than the fact that He was, in the outcome, actually put to death; and let us consider afterwards whether the passion of Jesus, when thus set in the very centre of the Biblical picture, does in the end connect with our own experience of passion and invest it with a certain greatness, a certain dignity.

At a certain time Jesus appeared in Galilee preaching the good news of the Kingdom of God. He appeared publicly but with no more publicity, in the modern sense of the word, than would attend any other Rabbi of that period. Jesus became known by rumour and report of His works of healing and His vivid and confident teaching; but no doubt the rumours and reports of Him were often received with scepticism by those who heard them or dismissed as the idle gossip of the peasantry. We are not to suppose that from the outset of His public ministry Jesus achieved national fame or notoriety.

His preaching of the reality and presence of God's Kingdom was described as 'good news'; but it was news which invited and required a certain kind of response. It invited the hearers to discipleship of the Kingdom—to a way of life which included, for some, the abandonment of home and occupation and constant presence in Jesus' company and involved, for all, a trustful relationship with God which, in the dealings of man with man, would overcome covetousness and vindictiveness and arrogance and envy. So Jesus preached and taught; and He gathered a circle and following of more or less committed disciples.

But the way of the Kingdom which He preached was not the way for individuals only: it was also the way for Israel— for His own beloved, God-chosen nation. The way of the nation in its public stance and policy, no less than the way of the individual in his private affairs, was to be the way of the Kingdom: the nation itself must be won to discipleship of

79

the Kingdom. And this meant that the leaders of the nation must be won. Jesus was no political revolutionary, bent on transferrring the national leadership into other hands or seizing it for Himself: the revolution which was His goal was a revolution in the hearts and understanding of men, including those men who exercised political power and national leadership. These men, like the peasants of Galilee, must be invited and won to discipleship of the Kingdom.

So at a certain time, when He had already won a considerable following, Jesus resolved to present Himself to the nation's leaders in the capital city; and He resolved to do so at Passover time—the time when there would be with Him in the capital the largest possible following of peasant-pilgrims from Galilee. He chose this time of set purpose: for the men He sought to invite and win to discipleship were political men, exercising responsibility for the nation, and such men will never take seriously a cause or appeal which is devoid of popular support. To such men the way of the Kingdom could be appealing only if it appeared *viable*, only if it could demonstrate its capacity to arouse enthusiasm and win support. If Jesus had presented Himself to the nation's leaders alone, a solitary eccentric with no evident support, His invitation to them would have been unappealing, unrealistic, even unfair: only evidence of a substantial following, enthusiastic and orderly, could possibly win the attention and discipleship of responsible politicians. So for the sake of the Kingdom, in order to offer to their nation's leaders the best, and perhaps the only, chance of becoming disciples of the Kingdom, Jesus presented Himself in Jerusalem when the strength of His following would be most evident; and we see Him as He enters the city by the Mount of Olives staging a modest demonstration which would make His presence in the city known and rally His followers to His side.

For the sake of the Kingdom, in order to win the nation to the way of the Kingdom, Jesus displayed before the nation's leaders the viability of that way. He offered to them the only argument that was likely to convince them—the argument that the way of the Kingdom was a practical possibility, capable of winning widespread support; and He presented this argument in concrete and visible form—in the actual presence in the capital of the maximum strength of His following. But in so doing He exposed Himself to a very great risk: for that which was intended to appeal to the nation's leaders could also be interpreted as a threat to them.

In the open-air civilization of Mediterranean countries the crowds in the streets of capital cities have always contained a potential threat to stable government. In the last days of the Roman republic the volatility of the Roman 'mob' made the state ungovernable; and when the imperial system was erected upon the ruins of the republic there was no firmer element in imperial policy than the preservation of order in the streets of major cities. In the provinces subjected to Roman rule, local leadership was used to maintain the peace, and was supported or tolerated just to the extent that peace *was* maintained. So it was in Judaea. A measure of authority and autonomy was permitted to the Jewish leadership so long as peace was maintained, so long as the streets were quiet; but if disturbances broke out the immediate effect would be either the replacement of the local leaders or the abolition of local leadership and 'direct rule' by Rome. Disturbance in the streets of Jerusalem would have as its first consequence the loss of power and position by the Jewish leaders.

Roman government was rarely concerned with the rights and wrongs, the cause or justification, of such disturbance: that it happened was enough to bring down, or at least to threaten, local leadership. So we see immediately why the presence of Jesus and His following in Jerusalem at Passover-time could be read as a threat by the Jewish leaders. It was not that they had reason to suppose that He intended 'to overthrow the government'. It was simply that the presence in the city at that time of a popular and striking leader accompanied by a numerous following would be 'exciting', and therefore possibly 'disturbing', and therefore potentially 'threatening'. The evident strength of the way of the Kingdom, which might appeal to the Jewish leaders and win them to discipleship, might also be read by them as a threat and provoke them to a pre-emptive reaction. The more effectively Jesus *appealed* to the nation's leaders by displaying the strength of His support, the more dangerously He might be taken to *threaten*; and in seeming to threaten He exposed Himself to the danger of a decisive and violent reaction. The very initiative which was most likely to win the nation's leaders to discipleship of the Kingdom was also most likely to make them the executioners of Jesus: the outcome, very finely balanced, must depend entirely on their decision.

This Jesus knew well: as He deliberately made His last journey to Jerusalem He knew that the possible, and even the probable, outcome of this journey would be His death. For this probability He prepared both Himself and His disciples. Of the other possibility—that He would live to see the nation's leaders won to discipleship—He did not speak lest He should be tempted by it—tempted, that is to say, to behave 'discreetly' in Jerusalem, to 'adopt a low profile', to diminish the threat which He presented by concealing the power of His own personality and the strength of His support. But such a policy would diminish also the appeal of the way of the Kingdom to political men: it would save Jesus' life but harm the cause of the Kingdom.

Therefore, lest He should be tempted by this safer but less effective policy, Jesus gave no thought to the possibility that He might live. His words as He approached the city were of His impending death; and His followers, looking back on what He had said, believed that He already knew for a certainty that He would die. But even this is not to say that He willed or intended to die—that He did what He did in order to bring about His death. His will was for the cause of the Kingdom; and the cause of the Kingdom was to be advanced not by His death as such but by His exposure 'unto death'— by the creation of a situation of which the issue, depending on the response of the nation's leaders, must be either the triumph of the Kingdom or His own elimination, His own death. Jesus handed Himself over 'unto death'—as any man does who, in the cause of some great good, exposes himself to the probable loss of everything, even his own life; and Jesus willed to be so handed over because there was no other way in which the appeal of the Kingdom could be so powerfully and realistically presented to the nation's leaders.

So Jesus willed, and so He acted—appearing publicly in Jerusalem, speaking boldly, concealing neither the force of His personality nor the strength of His following, making it possible that the nation's leaders would be attracted by the cause of the Kingdom, making it probable that they would feel threatened and react with violence. One might say that by His presence and manner in Jerusalem Jesus so raised the stakes that the Jewish leaders must become either his disciples or his executioners: the possibility of a response less dramatic and decisive was excluded.

There came a time when Jesus became aware that one of His close followers was negotiating with the Jewish authorities—arranging what would be called today a 'confrontation' in which their response would become evident. Perhaps, as yet, Jesus knew no more than this. Perhaps He did not yet know with certainty the spirit in which the negotiations were being conducted; perhaps He did not yet know with certainty what the response would be. But He knew that the moment of decision, the moment of truth, was about to come; and, having completed His work, having done all that could be done to win the nation to the way of the Kingdom, He went to the Garden of Gethsemane to wait upon the outcome.

Waiting can be the most intense and poignant of all human experiences—the experience which, above all others, strips us of affectation and self-deception and reveals to us the reality of our needs, our values and ourselves. Waiting is at its most intense and wearing when it takes one or other of two particular forms. Sometimes we wait with dread for the onset or occurrence of something which, with our rational faculties, we know to be necessary or appropriate or even beneficial to ourselves. So a nervous actor may wait for the curtain to rise or a paratrooper for the moment when he must make his first jump: so many of us wait in the dentist's waiting room. We dread the imminent onset of strain or danger or pain, but we know with our rational faculties that what lies ahead is 'for

83

the best'. Usually rational considerations overcome dread and we do not 'run away'. We count it weakness or cowardice if we do; and we also count it weakness if, as we wait, we find ourselves hoping or praying that that which lies ahead—that which is 'for the best'—may not happen: that the performance on the stage may be cancelled, that bad weather may prevent the parachute jump, that the dentist may find himself too busy to see us. There is weakness—pardonable weakness but nevertheless weakness—in hoping or praying to be 'spared' that which we know to be for the best. Air-crews about to embark on a particularly dangerous mission in war-time may sometimes hope or pray that their allotted aircraft may prove unserviceable; but few if any would admit at the time to doing so.

Now we must notice that, according to some interpretations of the purpose of Jesus, He experienced such weakness, albeit momentarily, in the Garden of Gethsemane. He had come to Jerusalem in order to die—in order to achieve by His death God's purpose and His own. That He should die was, in this sense, 'for the best'; and yet, as He waited in dread in Gethsemane, He prayed, momentarily, that He might be 'spared'— that the cup might pass from Him.

But, as we have said, there is another form of peculiarly intense and poignant waiting. It is the manner of waiting in which the prisoner in the dock—or the prisoner's wife or mother—waits for the jury to announce their verdict; the manner in which an intelligent man waits for the surgeon's report on a biopsy of his liver; the manner in which, after an explosion in a coalmine, a wife waits at the pit-head to hear if her own man is safe. One waits at such moments in an agonizing tension between hope and dread, stretched and almost torn apart between two dramatically different anticipations. A wise person will then steel and prepare himself for the worst; but the very tension in which he waits shows that hope is still present, and that hope will often express itself, even in unbelievers, in the urgent and secret prayer, 'O God, let it be all right'. In such hope and prayer there is no weakness, no failure of nerve: torn between rational hope and rational dread one may properly pray for the best while still prepared for the worst.

Perhaps it was in such a manner that Jesus waited and prayed in His agony in the Garden. Already He had done, at His own immense risk, all that could be done for the cause of the Kingdom, to win the nation to discipleship. Already He had achieved His purpose—He had handed Himself over 'unto death'. Now, through Judas' arrangement, the confrontation was about to come, the dénouement was about to appear. Jesus knew that the men of power, or their representatives, would come to the Garden: but *how* would they come—as disciples or as executioners? Once on another night, according to John's Gospel, one of them, Nicodemus, had come as a disciple; and Jesus' prayer 'let this cup pass from me' perhaps breathes the urgent, slender, yet proper hope that they might all so come on this night. We are told that Jesus posted Peter and James and John to 'watch' in the Garden; and one asks oneself what they were to watch for, why they were to watch. Were they to tell Jesus, when the time came, *that* they were coming? Or were they to tell Him *how* they were coming? It seems, in fact, that they told Him neither; and it was the appearance of weapons in the Garden, of swords and staves, which told the truth, which disclosed the dénouement, which revealed to Jesus that He was indeed to drink the cup of death.

Now events took their course. The action passed into the hands of the nation's leaders and their agents and associates. Jesus did nothing more. There was nothing more than He *could* do: for already He had done all that *could* be done to win those men to discipleship of the Kingdom. Already, for that purpose, He had exposed Himself 'unto death'. Now He must simply wait upon and receive whatever was done to Him; and that which was done to Him culminated, as He had foreseen, in His death.

In telling the story of Jesus in this way we see Him as One Who, for a great good, exposes Himself to the extremity of risk. For the sake of a great good He creates a situation of which the outcome does not lie in His own hands and may be infinitely costly and painful and destructive to Himself. The story we have told implies that Jesus *expected* to be put to death—and perhaps this expectation was grounded not only in the rational judgement that His appeal to the nation's leader was more likely than not to be taken as a threat but also in His memory of prophetic words about a Servant who, for the sake of the people, was destined to be scorned and chastised and put to death. But the story does not imply that Jesus willed His death or purposed His death as an end in itself or as in itself a benefit to the nation or a blessing to mankind. Therefore, in telling the story of Jesus in this way we are delivered from certain difficulties. We do not need to ascribe 'weakness' to Jesus at that moment when He prayed in the Garden that He might be spared from death. We do not need to attribute to physical death those powerfully beneficial effects which are presupposed in certain societies but extremely difficult to accept in our own day. We give no countenance to the suggestion, or accusation, that the death of Jesus was 'a kind of suicide' or that, by willing His death at the hands of men, He imposed upon those men the sin and guilt of murder. In the present age when all too many are courting martyrdom in order to heap guilt or opprobrium upon their opponents it seems especially important that the story of Jesus should be told in such a way as leaves no room for the possibility that He also was 'courting death'.

Jesus' purpose was to spare nothing, not even His own life, in the cause of winning the nation to discipleship of the Kingdom. He sought from the nation's leaders that which could not be compelled—the response of discipleship; and He sought it with such earnestness as to create a situation in which there could be no temporizing or ambiguous response on their part. Faced in the streets of the capital by the strength of Jesus' following they must become either His disciples or His executioners. What lay in their hands, what depended on their response, was not whether Jesus should be tolerantly heard or rudely rebuffed: it was whether He should be followed in the way of the Kingdom or totally eliminated from the scene. So, through the initiative which Jesus Himself took and the situation which He Himself created, He handed Himself over without limit or reserve—'unto death'. He entered into the totality or extremity of passion—the situation in which there is no limit to what may be done to one, to what one may receive or suffer; and at the great climax of the story, at the moment when He is handed over in the Garden, we see Him waiting, in the agony of expectancy, for whatever it is that He is to receive.

# 6

# The God Who Waits

In the last chapter we have told the story of Jesus in such a way that the climax of it is reached in His passion rather than in His death, and—if the distinction may be permitted—the critical scene is set in the Garden of Gethsemane rather than on the Hill of Calvary. It is the scene in Gethsemane, with its agony of waiting, which is the logical and inevitable consequence of what Jesus has done and purposed: it is to this that, by His own will, He has destined Himself. What follows, what is actually done to Him, is determined not by His own will but by the response of men—of sinful men, concerned for their own prestige and position—to the choice which He has set before them. The exercise of Jesus' will, of His activity and initiative and purpose, comes to an end in the waiting in the Garden.

That Jesus waited in that particular place was the outcome of the arrangements and the deed of Judas; but that He should wait in *some* place for the response of the nation's leaders was the inevitable and necessary outcome of His own activity and purpose. It was not through the accident of what Judas did that He passed into the hands of men, nor yet through any misjudgement or miscalculation on His own part. Nor yet was it through the inherent weakness of His own position—the weakness of the individual *vis-à-vis* the state. One must suppose that, as a wandering Rabbi teaching the way of the Kingdom in the villages of Galilee, Jesus would have been no more exposed than any other man of His time. What exposed Him 'unto death' was His own initiative in presenting the way of the Kingdom so powerfully that if its appeal was not accepted it must be received as deadly threat. Jesus was exposed 'unto death' not through inherent weakness but through the exercise of strength. No weak and wandering Rabbi could either have appealed to the nation's leaders or threatened them as Jesus did: it was from a position of strength and not of weakness that He passed, by His own initiative, into the hands of men.

Now we have seen that in John's Gospel this transition, this passing into the hands of men, is the moment at which, above every other moment, the presence of God and the glory of God is evident in Jesus. It is at this moment that He uses of Himself words which *are* the Name of God; and it is at this moment that men fall to the ground before Him. It is not through the teaching of Jesus nor through His mighty works that the deepest dimension of the divine glory is disclosed in Jesus and that men are overwhelmed by the divine presence: it is through the fact that, of His own will, He places Himself in men's hands and becomes exposed to whatever they will do. So John, in his characteristic way, seems to suggest; and the suggestion is of the greatest importance. For if it is true, then Jesus, in handing Himself over, in passing of His own will from action to passion, enacts and discloses that which, at the deepest level, is distinctive of divinity, distinctive of God. He discloses the God Who Himself, of His own will, is handed over to pass from action to passion.

At this point we must clearly revert to that doctrine of the impassibility of God to which we referred at the end of the fourth chapter. How can *that* doctrine possibly be sustained against *this* disclosure? Must it not be totally discarded? Must it not be dismissed as alien to 'the truth which is in Jesus'— the truth which is manifested in the Garden of Gethsemane at the climax of the story of Jesus? Must it not be branded as an instance of the improper influence of Greek philosophical thought upon the development and formulation of Christian theology?

To this question we now turn. Let us note first that the Latin termination *-ibilis* (or *-abilis*) and the English termination '-ible' (or '-able') derived from it refer rather to what is to be expected than to what is in fact the case. If a man's behaviour is 'laudable' or 'culpable' he will expect to be praised or blamed: it will be natural and proper that he should be praised or blamed. But it does not follow that he will in fact be praised or blamed. If we describe a child as 'unlovable' we suggest that he or she is not likely to be loved; but we do not imply that the child never has been and never will be loved. It would be no offence either against language or against logic to say that an unlovable child was deeply loved. Admirable people are not always admired and pardonable errors are not always pardoned. Unpardonable insults are sometimes forgiven, inviolable treaties are sometimes broken, intolerable burdens are sometimes borne by exceptionally strong people and incredible stories are sometimes believed by exceptionally foolish people. To say that a story is incredible is not to say that no one believes it: it is to say that it is not likely, not fitting, not in the nature of things that it should be believed.

The suffix we are considering points, we repeat, to what is to be expected rather than to what is in fact the case. It suggests that a person or thing is *of such a nature as* to be loved or not loved, pardoned or not pardoned, believed or not believed. So when we hear that an unlovable person is in fact loved we are faced not with a logical contradiction but with what is, in the correct and literal sense of the word, a paradox—with something that confounds or contradicts our reasonable expectations. The paradoxical statement that the person is loved does not formally contradict the statement that he is unlovable: what it contradicts is our reasonable and well-grounded expectation in the matter. Having heard and accepted that—to our surprise—the person is loved we may still insist, without logical contradiction, that he is unlovable.

Let us carry the matter one stage further. Expectations which are reasonable and justifiable are often connected with, or emerge out of, an awareness of 'rights'. An admirable man has a certain right to be admired; and a man who commits an unpardonable offence has no right to pardon. Rights may be invaded or ignored but they are not thereby abrogated;

and so a person whom no one at all admires may still be admirable, and a person whom everyone blames may not, in fact, be culpable. A person retains his legal and moral rights even when they are ignored by others. But there are certain occasions when someone, by his own will and initiative, surrenders his rights or transfers those rights to others. So a diplomat may surrender his immunity from prosecution; a parent who is not liable for the debts of an adult son may accept liability; a Minister of the Crown may accept responsibility for the errors of a subordinate. This 'surrender' or 'acceptance' is no mere gesture, no mere posture to be amended if the consequences prove unpleasant: the diplomat really will have to appear in court, the parent really will have to pay the debt, the Minister really will hear calls for his resignation. Nevertheless in speaking of such cases we should probably want to distinguish them from the case of the foreign resident who has no immunity from prosecution and of the person who is sued for his own debts and the Minister who is criticized for his own errors: certainly it would be misleading to say without qualification that the diplomat was open to prosecution, the parent liable for the sum in question or the Minister responsible for the error in question. To describe the situation correctly we should need to mention both the 'rights' of the people concerned and the facts that they themselves had surrendered or transferred those rights.

With these preliminaries let us now return to the Christian doctrine of the impassibility of God. Let us consider the opposite possibility. Let us imagine that the Christian Church had announced in the past, or should announce now, that God is 'passible'. This would imply that it is 'in the nature of things' that God should be exposed to or affected by or dependent upon that which happens in the world: that it is to be expected that God should be the object no less than the subject of that which happens in the world. The description of God as passible would imply a relationship of mutuality or fundamental interdependence between God and the world: it would imply that just as God is necessary to what the world is, so the world is necessary to what God is. If God is in His nature passible, then without the world He is, in one aspect of His being, incomplete: He must need the world in order that the passible, affective, receptive aspect of His nature may be fulfilled.

Statements of this kind about the fundamental relationship, actual or conceivable, between God and the world often seem so far removed from our real and existential concerns that they command neither assent nor dissent. At best they are 'left to theologians'. But it does not require a theologian to discern two things. The first is that, if God and the world are seen as interdependent, as mutually necessary, then the concept of God loses all distinctness. God and the world become merged into one complex, interacting reality; and the differentiation of one part of that reality as 'God' becomes almost arbitrary. It becomes as arbitrary as it would be to differentiate one part of a complex machine or system as its 'God'. If it is in the nature of things that God should be dependent upon or affected by the world then God is, in truth, no more than 'part of the system'.

The second thing that can be discerned without any particular theological expertise is that, if God is seen as part of the system, He will be treated as part of the system. Man will see himself as having a claim on God of the same order as God's claim on him—the claim that each is necessary to the other—and he will have no less justification for exploiting the passibility and manipulating the power of God than he has for exploiting and manipulating the speed of the horse or the strength of the ox, the food value of grain or the energy of coal. Now the conviction that God is not to be exploited or manipulated is perhaps that which most sharply differentiates the major religions of mankind from the more 'primitive' or 'superstitious' forms of religious belief; and if Christianity—or any of the major religious systems—should abandon this conviction it is likely enough that it would survive only as a questionable system of magical manipulation. If Christianity had not been built upon the fundamental concepts of the sovereignty, the majesty, the 'otherness' of God, it is improbable that it would exist at the present time; and if these foundations should now be removed or undermined its survival with any resemblance to its original and traditional form would be most unlikely.

It seems therefore that the doctrine of the impassibility of God preserves and articulates a truth of fundamental importance—namely, that God is beyond manipulation or exploitation, that there is in Him no such 'dependence' upon the world that He can be constrained or compelled by the forces of nature, the aspirations of men or any other power or factor within the world. To deny this truth, to accept the superficially appealing possibility that God is 'just like us'—passible, dependent, 'human'—would be to pave the way for the degeneration of the Christian religion into some kind of magical and manipulative cult. It must be firmly maintained that God is impassible: that it is by no means 'in the nature of things' that God should be in any way dependent upon, exposed to or affected by the world: that it is the nature of God always to be the active and initiating subject, never the receptive object.

God is not passible. But in reflecting on the precise force and significance of the suffix '-ible' we have discerned the possibility of paradox: the possibility that the unlovable person may in fact be loved or that a person who is not responsible may 'take the blame'. The person who takes the blame is not obliged by external factors, by what has actually happened, to answer for a debt or an error; but by the exercise of his own initiative and freedom he obliges himself to do so. By the exercise of his freedom he surrenders his freedom and takes upon himself a constraint. To the paradox presented by such a person we cannot do justice either by a simple assertion of his responsibility or by a simple denial of it; and our phrase—that he has taken the blame—amounts to both a qualified assertion and a qualified denial of his responsibility.

The disclosure of God in Jesus seems to demand from Christian believers a similar kind of complex and paradoxical assertion. In the light of that disclosure neither a simple assertion nor a simple denial of the passibility of God is an adequate expression of the truth. The glory of God appears

93

in Jesus not simply in the fact that He is the initiating subject of activity, working in unfettered freedom, nor yet in the fact that He is the passive and receptive object of that which is done to Him, but in the fact that, of His own will and purpose, He passes from the former condition to the latter. It is not 'in the nature of things' that Jesus should be exposed 'unto death' to the decisions and deeds of men: it is of His own initiative and purpose that He is handed over to be so exposed; and it is that transition itself, that willed exchange of impassibility for passion, which decisively discloses His divinity—the glory of God in Him. It is not easy to find an English phrase which will contain the paradoxical meaning of this disclosure, but in Latin a phrase lies ready to hand. A Christian who, like John, discerns the glory of God in the handing over of Jesus will be driven to say, *Deus non passibilis sed passus*.

As we have seen, the phrase involves no logical contradiction. Nor does it involve any suggestion that the free activity of God can be affected or constrained by the existence or power of an 'other'—namely, of the world. God is not passible. But there is disclosed in Jesus a free activity of God which culminates in the surrender of freedom, in the handing over of Himself, in a willed transition to passion. Jesus destines Himself, by His own will, to wait upon the decisions and deeds of men: He works, one might say, towards a climax in which He must wait. If the truth of God is disclosed and the glory of God is manifest in Jesus, then the truth of God must be this, and the glory of God must appear in this—that God so initiates and acts that He destines Himself to enter into passion, to wait and to receive.

*Deus non passibilis sed passus*: of His own will and freedom God so acts as to enter into passion, to encompass His own passion. This, as John sees it, is the truth of God, and it is in this that the glory of God is manifested at its deepest level. The glory of God is disclosed at its primary level in the work and activity of God; but that glory appears at its deepest level when the activity of God achieves the exposure of God, when by His working God destines Himself to the necessity of waiting. One might say that the ultimate glory of God's creativity is the creation of His own exposure to that which He has created: that of all that God has done in and for the world the most glorious thing is this—that He has handed Himself over to the world, that He has given to the world not only power of being but also that power to affect Himself which is best described as power of meaning. Of such a nature is that ultimate dimension of divine glory which is disclosed in the handing over of Jesus.

John tells of men falling to the ground when, at the moment when Jesus is handed over, the deepest dimension of divine glory is disclosed to them. In what they do the men bear witness to what they see; but no doubt we are to understand that these particular men do so unwittingly, with no real comprehension, with no more than a passing flash of insight or recognition. But what these men do surely implies what John himself believes and what is presupposed or asserted in all his writing—namely, that 'we beheld His glory', that that dimension of divine glory which appears in the Son of God is not wholly unrecognizable by the eyes of men nor wholly incomprehensible by their minds. The divine glory over-whelms, but it does not simply bemuse or bewilder; nor does it terrify. Man has some capacity, however imperfect, for recognizing 'the majesty of His glory': some element within his own experience which prepares him to kneel rather than to flee when the divine glory is manifested, to bow himself in reverence rather than to hide himself in terror. In the eyes of John the glory of God disclosed in the handing over of Jesus is, so to speak, of a familiar shape though on an unfamiliar scale; and in the end, in his later reflection, John is moved to identify and describe that shape in a very familiar word.

It can be no coincidence that the writer who in his Gospel most clearly discerns the glory of God in the handing over of Jesus is also the writer who, in the first of his Epistles, makes the memorable declaration that 'God is love'. For love, as it is known imperfectly and fragmentarily in human experience, is of precisely the 'shape' which John discerns in the life of Jesus. Love acts of its own initiative, under no compulsion or constraint, in order that another may benefit; and the activity

95

which is characteristic of love is, in principle, without limit or qualification. In loving one offers no limited proportion of what one has and is: one expends, or at least makes available, the whole of one's resources. But this unlimited expenditure is made for the sake of an other—in order that an other may receive; and, whenever that other is no mere extension of oneself but truly an other, then it must remain in doubt whether that other will in fact receive. In authentic loving there is no control of the other who is loved: that he or she will receive is beyond the power of love to ordain or know. So when our work of love is done we are destined to wait upon the outcome—to wait upon the response of acceptance or rejection, of understanding or misunderstanding, which either fulfills our own activity or makes it vain. By our activity of loving we destine ourselves, in the end, to waiting—to placing in the hands of an other the outcome of our own endeavour and to exposing ourselves to receive from those hands the triumph or tragedy of our own endeavour. Through our own initiative in loving we create a situation of which the issue passes out of our hands: we place what is done or given in other hands to be accepted or rejected. And since what is done or given in authentic love is without limit or qualification, it is in fact ourselves and our own destiny that we place in other hands. When we love we hand ourselves over to receive from an other our own triumph or our own tragedy.

Where love is, action is destined to pass into passion: working into waiting. The intimate connection between loving and waiting is expressed in familiar and popular ways in the representation of the lover as a *waiting* figure—waiting on the corner, waiting for a letter, waiting beside the telephone; and the connection is made explicitly and powerfully in Dostoevsky's great novel *Crime and Punishment*. The hero—or anti-hero—of the novel, Raskolnikov, is a young man of powerful intelligence but stunted or non-existent feeling. He is a kind of voyeur of life—sharp in observation, distant and cold in emotion; capable of achieving, incapable of loving. Being a needy student, he comes to the conclusion that the wealth of a miserly old woman would be better employed in his hands than in hers; and, following the logic of his conclusion, he goes on to rob and murder her in cold blood.

The murder itself, and the physical brutality which it involves, proves somewhat disturbing to Raskolnikov: so also does the unexpected subtlety and intelligence of the prosecutor who investigates the crime. Raskolnikov is surprised and upset by his arrest and conviction and incarceration in a prison camp in Siberia; but his fundamental detachment remains, and he responds with hardly more than irritation to the comfort and encouragement offered by his family and friends.

Among his friends is the girl Sonia Marmeladov, who loves him and in the end follows him to Siberia. Each day, when the prisoners are allowed an hour of exercise near the prison fence, Sonia comes to the fence and talks to Raskolnikov and gives him small gifts. But he is still cool, distant, unresponsive to Sonia's devotion and love; and he loiters by the prison fence rather as a matter of daily routine than for the pleasure of seeing her or the opportunity of speaking with her.

Sonia falls ill and for several weeks is unable to come to the fence. Raskolnikov, of course, loiters there as usual, scarcely affected by her absence. But eventually Sonia recovers; and on a certain morning she sends word to Raskolnikov through another prisoner that she will probably come to the fence that same afternoon. When the hour of exercise comes, Raskolnikov finds himself as usual beside the fence—wandering up and down, mooching, loitering. And then suddenly, in one vivid moment, he realizes that on this particular day he is not loitering but waiting—waiting upon Sonia's coming, waiting for her to come or not to come. And in this moment when he finds himself *waiting* for Sonia, Raskolnikov realizes that he loves her. He who has never loved before discovers in the awareness of waiting the awareness of loving; and Dostoevsky describes this new-found awareness as Raskolnikov's entry into life, his 'resurrection'.

In the light of his resurrection Raskolnikov's earlier detachment appears to the reader—and even to himself—as an inadequacy. His earlier image of himself as a free man, controlling his own destiny, impervious to the actions, opinions and affections of others, collapses in the end; and its collapse is recognized even by Raskolnikov himself not as tragedy but as triumph. For in its place there appears the image of a man whose new-found dependence and helplessness is the dependence and helplessness of love. Raskolnikov must wait upon Sonia's coming because now he loves her; and so the necessity of waiting lifts him into what can only be called a new dimension of living. In the perspective of one who has begun to love the earlier freedom, detachment and independence become of no account; and the loss of them appears as gain. Perhaps they were not contemptible in themselves; but now they are outshone in moral worth and existential power by that particular form of dependence which consists in loving an other and waiting upon that other's response. Raskolnikov's resurrection is repeated in miniature in every person who, having cultivated and 'gloried in' an independent style of life, falls in love and finds himself or herself disturbingly aware of a new dimension of glory.

This is a familiar experience—that when one loves life enters a new dimension of 'glorious' possibility. This is recognizable from the outside as well as from the inside; and it is recognizable at the most ordinary and commonplace level. The man who 'has no ties', 'who has only himself to please', may for that reason be found particularly sociable or obliging or useful; but one would scarcely admire or respect him for his independence. One might feel a moment of passing envy or express a jocular congratulation; but no parent who has loved would wish a son or daughter to go through life in that kind of 'freedom'—without loving and without the dependence that comes of loving. We know that loving involves dependence and exposure and may in consequence be painful and tragic to the one who loves; but we should not wish a son or daughter or anyone for whom we care to go through life shielded or inhibited from such exposure. A life so shielded would be diminished, a two-dimensional life; and, however successful in its own terms, it would seem, from the perspective of those who know what it is to love, scarcely worth living. If a person has never loved, then, however successful his life has been in other ways, we feel a certain cool pity—for the fact that his life has been so 'empty': if a person has loved, however tragically, we cannot but feel a certain admiration, and if we weep for him our tears are of sympathy and not of pity.

Ordinary life, the life of man through the ages, discloses to us, in the experience of loving, this dimension of glory—discloses the transcendence of loving over everything else that a human being can do. The Gospel of John suggests to us that the divine glory, in that ultimate dimension in which it appears in the handing over of Jesus, is of this same shape, though on a vaster scale. There is in it something whose shape we know and can recognize—the shape of the glory of loving. There is in the God Who is disclosed in Jesus first the glory of signs and mighty works—the glory of free and unfettered activity and achievement; but when Jesus destines himself, by His own will and initiative, to wait at the end in exposure and helplessness, there is disclosed, as the ultimate dimension of the divine glory, that same glory which we dimly perceive in our own experience when, because we love, we destine ourselves to wait and to be exposed and to receive. The glory of that waiting figure in Gethsemane is not *wholly* strange and unfamiliar to us—not so strange that we could mistake it for misfortune and regard the figure with pity or sheer incomprehension. The glory of God which finally appears in the waiting figure in the Garden is the glory of that not wholly unfamiliar activity which always, in the end, destines itself to waiting—the activity of loving.

So we perceive that the ultimate dimension of the glory of God lies in that activity which creates, in the end, its own passion; in that working which, in the end, destines itself to waiting. The most glorious activity of God is that He hands Himself over, and, in His free activity of loving, surrenders His own impassibility. God is indeed *actus purus*—pure activity; but within the range of the divine activity is the activity of self-exposure, the activity of destining oneself to wait upon that which one has made and to receive from that to which

99

one has given the power to be. The supreme, most glorious activity of God is that He gives to that which He makes power of meaning—power to mean something to himself, power to be the subject over against Himself as the object. The image of God in which man is made is the image of *this* God—Who, in loving, exposes Himself to be the object no less than the subject of that which happens in the world; and so the presence of the image of God in man is, in principle, to be discerned no less in his passion than in his activity and achievement. Man is, in principle, no less 'god-like' when he is waiting upon the world than when he is working upon, and achieving within, the world.

As we have suggested, we tend to recognize this truth when the waiting of man, his passion and dependence, is evidently and obviously the outcome of his loving. In the parable of the Prodgial Son the good father, eagerly waiting for any sign or glimpse of his son's return, is both a very human figure and a very 'god-like' figure; and in anyone who waits as he waited, in the passion of love, we have no difficulty in recognizing a great and even 'god-like' dignity. But in earlier chapters of this book we have been considering human experiences of dependence and helplessness which are simply forced upon us and have no evident connection with loving—the waiting of the patient upon the hospital bed, of the old man in need of help, of the worker held up for lack of power or information, of a driver in a stationary queue of traffic. The question therefore which remains and to which we must now turn is whether in waiting of this commonplace kind there is merely a diminution of man's dignity and an affront to the divine image which he bears, or whether here also there may be something appropriate to man's unique status in the world, something through which the divine image may still be discerned in him.

# 7

# The Stature of Waiting

We noticed earlier that in the contemporary world activity tends to be valued for its own sake. We encourage children to be 'busy' and applaud elderly people for 'keeping active'; and this encouragement and applause has little to do with the worth, in beauty or utility, of what emerges from their activity. Activity which is quite unproductive in terms of beauty or utility is nevertheless generally respected: indeed one observes a growing respect for a form of activity which, by its very nature, neither has nor is intended to have any valuable 'product'—the activity of 'play'.

Now it may be of course that unproductive activity is respected simply because it develops or preserves the skills and habits which may be used at other times in creative and productive ways; but one gets the impression that the roots of our respect go rather deeper than this. After all, the elderly person who expresses the hope of 'being active to the end' is patently not thinking of that unending activity as preparation or training for some yet further and more productive activity; and the person who says—and is generally applauded for saying—'I am only happy when I have something to do' clearly does not feel that his or her 'doing' is in need of justification by its useful and productive consequences.

It seems that the dignity which we discern in productive and creative activity tends to impart itself to *all* forms of activity—or at least to all which are not positively harmful or destructive. Because 'doing' can be productive, creative and, as such, appropriate to the divine image which we bear, all forms of activity tend, as it were, to be 'sanctified' and judged worthy of our human condition—even the activity of play. Our public attitude is that to be fully human, to be alive in a fully human sense, is to be active—even if our activity has no end or goal beyond itself, no worthwhile or useful effect.

We have argued in previous chapters that the divine image which we bear may be an image of passion no less than of action; for the God Who is disclosed in Jesus is the One Who hands Himself over to be affected by the world, to receive the impact and the meaning of the world, to wait upon the world. It is of this God that we bear the image—an image that includes passion no less than action, waiting no less than working. Now within our human experience there is one kind or occasion of waiting in which it is not too difficult to discern at least the faint image of the God Who waits; and that is the waiting to which we destine ourselves by loving. In the human figure who, because he loves, finds himself exposed and vulnerable to what may be done to him, waiting upon what may be done to him, the image of the God Who is disclosed in Jesus is not unrecognizable: one might almost say that that figure seems a 'holy' figure. But does the 'holiness' of waiting in love extend to other forms of waiting? Does it, and can it, impart a kind of 'sanctity' to other and more commonplace forms of waiting? Can we perceive in the waiting figure in general any vestige of the image of the God Who is disclosed in Jesus?

Let us notice first that *any* kind of waiting presupposes some kind or degree of *caring*. One cannot be said to wait for or upon something which is a matter of indifference. If a down-and-out is taking shelter in a railway station, many trains may arrive while he is there; but he is not waiting for any of them. The only people waiting for the trains are those to whom the arrival of one or more trains matters, to whom it is in some sense important that one or more of the trains should arrive. To different people who are waiting the arrival of a particular train may be important for different reasons— to one because he expects his wife to be on it, to another because he must load mail-bags onto it; but unless its arrival is in some way important to a person he cannot be said to be waiting for it. It follows that a person to whom few things are important rarely waits. A person who views the world with indifference rarely finds himself waiting. Conversely a person to whom many things matter will often find himself waiting. The experience of waiting is the experience of the world as in some sense *mattering*, as being of some kind of importance.

There comes to mind a visit to a hospital long ago to see a young man, John, who was in a severely depressed or possibly schizophrenic condition. The charge-nurse knew that I was coming and said, 'I have brought John into the day-room: he is waiting for you there.' John was indeed in the day-room; but I soon became aware that he was not waiting—for me or for anyone or anything else. When I entered the room he continued to look at the chairs and walls with a wandering, indifferent gaze; and when I sat directly in front of him he looked through me and round me rather than at me. I offered him a parcel of fruit, but he did not lift a finger to take it; and when I put it on the chair beside him he did not touch it. I asked him questions, gave him news of friends, joked, appealed to him, spoke to him on every variety of subject in every variety of tone; but there came no response at all in word or expression. Still his eyes moved around with equal indifference over chairs and walls and windows and the picture on the television screen and myself and the fireplace and the nurse at the far end of the room. And yet he was certainly not unconscious or unaware of my presence or his surroundings; for once he addressed me correctly by name, and on two or three occasions he mentioned, dully but spontaneously and correctly, what he saw—that one window was open, that my coat was wet. It seemed that he was accurately aware of the world, registering it as correctly as anyone else, as correctly as a camera, but that nothing in the world mattered to him or possibly could matter. I received the disturbing impression that if I were to stand on my head or the nurse set fire to herself John would continue to look through and round and over us with expressionless eyes, and would, at the most, remark with dull indifference that I was upside-down or the nurse on fire.

John's condition was, of course, pathological and even-tuated sadly in his suicide some months later. But the ex-perience of being with him on that occasion brought home in a vivid and unforgettable way the possibility that man might exist with a merely camera-like consciousness, aware of the world but totally unmoved and unaffected by it, aware of everything but caring about nothing. No doubt man would not long survive in such a condition; but the condition is certainly imaginable—the condition in which man would per-ceive the world but perceive it with massive indifference, as irrelevant, as having no bearing on himself, no meaning for himself. In such a condition no man would ever wait. The man who waits is in a different condition. To him the world, or at least something in the world, presents itself as mattering: something in the world has power of meaning. At the opposite extreme to the case of John would be, for instance, that of a naturalist who waits, with extraordinary intensity, perhaps all night, for some ordinary but rarely observed event of the natural world—badger cubs coming out of the sett, the first flight of a young owl. To such a person such an event is worth waiting for. To many people it would be unimportant; but to the naturalist its happening, or failure to happen, will be an occasion, if not of triumph or tragedy, at least of great delight or disappointment.

The naturalist, through his interest in and care for nature, becomes exposed to delight or disappointment in the events of nature. One might even say that he is handed over, or hands himself over, to those events and to their power of meaning. The naturalist has probably been active, energetic and resourceful in discovering the sett or nest, constructing his hide and so on; but there comes a time when he must simply wait—when he must depend, for the outcome of his endeavour and for his own delight or disappointment, on that which is beyond control, on the creatures themselves.

The waiting figure of the naturalist crouched in his hide all night seems not wholly dissimilar from the waiting figure of the lover. Nor is it difficult to detect the same resemblance in the scientist or inventor who, having devised an experiment

104

which will be decisive for his theory, waits with extraordinary intensity for the result; or in the actor or performer who, having prepared with all possible diligence for his role, finds himself at last waiting in extreme tension for what will emerge from and through himself on the stage or platform; or in the artist who, as he works upon each brushstroke, is also waiting with concentrated intensity upon what will emerge from that stroke, both in itself and in relation to the composition as a whole. In such people we see figures totally handed over, for triumph or tragedy, to an outcome for which, having done all that can be done, they must simply wait.

It is by their venture of creativity that such people have handed themselves over and exposed themselves to waiting. It is of their own choice—or so at least it seems to other people—that they have become inventive scientists or creative artists. Their waiting, their final dependence on an outcome which is beyond their control, is, one might say, part and parcel of the adventure of creativity which is as glorious, as worthy of the image which man bears, as is the adventure of love. But such people form only a tiny proportion of those who wait. Much of the waiting with which we were concerned in earlier chapters seems of a quite different order from theirs. It is involuntary and seemingly no part of any adventure. It is simply imposed upon us by the way the world is and, in particular, by what the world has become in recent years. What glory is there, what trace of the divine image, in that figure who, through no choice of his own, lies helpless upon a hospital bed, monitored by machines, assessed by doctors, attended by nurses, visited or neglected by friends—that figure who, in his status of patient, seems to typify ever more precisely the condition of man in the present and future world?

Now in a certain sense, of course, that patient is where he is by his own choice. At some stage, because he felt ill, he went to the doctor and accepted the doctor's advice. Even if he was carried unconscious into hospital, he might, on recovering consciousness, have crawled out again or 'signed himself out' or refused treatment. In more general terms the dependence which is characteristic of the life of the individual today is not entirely and inevitably forced upon him: there is usually some way of 'opting out'. The frustrated worker may resign; the retired or unemployed person may refuse the provision that is made for him; the motorist trapped in a traffic jam may abandon his car and decline to drive again. We refrain from opting out not because it is physically impossible to do so but because we are aware of our needs, actual and potential. Our awareness of our fundamental needs—for relief of pain, for food and shelter, for some kind of company and ordered society—induces the great majority of us to remain 'within the system' and secure thereby the supply of our needs. We remain within the system because of our general awareness that we are not self-sufficient, that in the long run we cannot do without some measure of supply and support from outside ourselves.

Now when we recognize our need of this or that the outcome may be, on the one hand, resentment—a sense of personal indignity, of being defective or diminished. But it may on the other hand be appreciation—the recognition of the power or worth or quality of that which we need. When we become aware of our need of some commonplace commodity like water, the quality and power of that commodity sometimes appears remarkable. We perceive in water what we had not perceived before, and the commonplace commodity becomes a theme for poetry. During a spell in hospital we often become aware, as never before, of the kindness of people and of the importance of the small but necessary services which they perform; and Robinson Crusoe, marooned on his island, found his eyes opened to the extraordinary value both of the few simple tools and supplies which he had salvaged from the wreck and of those which he needed but lacked. Need or dependence can disclose not only our own deficiency but also—and often to remarkable degree—the power and value of people and things in the world around us. It is worth reflecting on the fact that it is in our period of greatest need, our infancy, that the roots are normally formed of that attention to the world, that sense of its relevance and importance, which is so sadly lacking in the schizophrenic. One might say that the fundamental deficiency of the schizophrenic is that he does not know his need of the world.

Through our awareness of needs we become exposed to powers and qualities in the world which otherwise perhaps would pass unrecognized. We become more aware of what the world is, of the heights and depths of existence. The awareness of need generates a sharper sensitivity or a wider receptivity which is not wholly unlike the sensitivity or receptivity of the lover or the artist. In the person who simply needs there is, admittedly, no prior exercise of will or initiative; but in so far as he is aware of his need he finds himself in the same situation as the artist or the lover. He also must wait; and in his waiting he is exposed to the power of meaning of that upon which he waits. The poignant dignity which we discern in the waiting figure of the lover or the artist is not wholly absent from the hungry man waiting to be fed or the patient waiting for relief of pain or even the commuter waiting for a delayed train. The need which constrains him to wait makes him also a point of heightened sensitivity, of more intense receptivity: in and through him *more is going on* than in the figure who, experiencing no need, has no concern—the figure who, in detachment, merely registers or records the world—the figure who appears in extreme form in the schizophrenic who waits for nothing and to whom nothing in the world has power of meaning.

To man in general there is given, through his awareness of need, something of that receptivity of the world to which the artist or the lover destines himself. Because we need the world, and know ourselves to need it, the world presents itself with power of meaning, as being of importance, as mattering. We do not merely register the world as the consciousness of the schizophrenic appears to register it: we find ourselves being drawn by the world or repelled by it, comforted or threatened, delighted or disappointed. To normal consciousness the world is not merely there: it 'means something to us'. And this power of meaning seems to have its roots in our awareness of our need of the world—our dependence on it for such basic necessities as food and shelter and company, for pleasure and relief of pain. In man's consciousness of such need seem to lie the roots and origins of the possibility that the world should 'mean something to him'.

So the power of meaning of the world is, in a sense, imposed upon us by our awareness of our needs. In certain religious traditions, from Buddhism to Stoicism, this imposition tends to be regarded as indeed an imposition—as a burden or degradation from which the wise and good man will strive to free himself. By ascetic discipline he will seek to rise above the physical and emotional needs which are the common lot of men; and in so doing he will also rise above the power of the world to affect himself. He will aspire to the condition which the Stoics called, significantly, *apatheia*—impassibility, invulnerability to and by the world. So he will come to see the world as—according to his theory—it is: meaningless, mere brute fact or even mere illusion. Freeing himself from need of the world he will achieve the viewpoint from which to perceive the world as it is—as meaningless chaos, as mere appearance, as illusion.

But this viewpoint and this perception of the world cannot be shared by anyone who has understood and accepted the disclosure of God which takes place in Jesus. For here is disclosed the God Who, creating the world in the activity of love, destines Himself to wait upon the world and gives to the world power of meaning to Himself. Because the world is created in love, it is invested with ultimate significance, with decisive power of meaning. So when man, through his awareness of need, perceives the world as mattering and receives its power of meaning, he perceives and receives no illusion but the truth. He perceives and receives the truth that 'the world means something'. This truth is indeed imposed upon him; for it is by man's common need and not only by his occasional aspiration as artist or lover that the world around him is invested with meaning. But the imposition of truth, when understood as such, will appear as gift or privilege rather than as burden. From the Christian viewpoint man's exposure to the power of meaning of the world is a gift from

God rather than an imposition by God: it is the communication to him, the sharing with him, of a fragment of that receptivity of the world which God, through loving the world, has created in Himself. Man, created in conscious dependence on the world, receives thereby a fragment of that impact or impress of the world which God, through loving the world, destines Himself to receive.

So when man waits upon the world—waits even for things so commonplace as food or sunrise or the relief of pain—the image of God is by no means absent from him or imperceptible in him. God also waits; and it is in waiting that He invests the world with the possibility and power of meaning. When man waits, even for the supply of commonplace needs, he is to that extent in a truly 'god-like' relationship to the world—a relationship no less 'god-like' than that in which he stands when he works upon the world and creates and achieves within the world. The image of God which is perceived in man's manifold capacity for activity within the world is to be perceived also in the range and variety of his capacity for passion—in the many ways and circumstances in which he waits upon the world: not only in the tense and 'holy' waiting to which the lover or artist destines himself by his own initiative in loving or creating, but in the various and commonplace forms of waiting which are 'imposed' upon us by our awareness of our various and commonplace needs.

The condition of waiting may obviously be physically pleasant or unpleasant. One may wait in an armchair for the beginning of a familiar and delightful programme on the television or one may wait on the rack for the next turn of the screw. And the condition may be emotionally pleasant or unpleasant: to wait with expectation for the coming of a birthday present is a very different matter from waiting with dread for the coming of a summons. Waiting, like activity, is, in itself, neither pleasant nor unpleasant. The point of our argument is not that waiting is never a disagreeable condition: it is that, from the Christian viewpoint, it is never a degraded condition, a condition of diminished human dignity. There is, we believe, in the Christian viewpoint an important corrective to the professed and public attitudes of today and to the presupposition on which they are based—the presupposition that human dignity is preserved only to the extent that man is active in the world, and initiates and creates and earns and achieves.

That a man should wait upon the attention of his fellow-men and depend upon them for help and service: that men should wait upon machines or depend upon systems: that one's daily bread should be provided rather than earned or achieved: that one should receive by gift rather than acquire by right: that one should lose one's independence: that one should wait upon the world rather than work upon it—all these notions and possibilities are to varying degrees repugnant to the public attitudes of the present day. And we are carrying such attitudes into a future in which, at least in the Western world, the possibilities of individual initiative and achievement are likely to become ever more restricted. We are, so to speak, pinning the flags of our values to a sinking ship. As we feel the ship sinking we exhort one another ever more earnestly to keep the flag flying—the flag of independence and individual enterprise and personal achievement and unceasing activism: and under these colours we sail courageously but perhaps ill-advisedly into a future in which, to an ever-increasing degree, the system will dominate the individual, machines will take over the work of men, our longer lives will be sustained by external support and the end-products of private initiative and activity will be of no more than sentimental value—the value of a bedraggled dishcloth knitted by an ancient lady who, from force of life-long habit, 'cannot bear to be doing nothing'.

Our values seem to be in conflict with our possibilities. Of course values are not to be surrendered at the first sign of difficulty in applying them. But when the difficulty of applying certain values appears insurmountable, it seems appropriate to reflect on these values—to scrutinize their origins and authenticity. We have suggested that the public values which prevail today—the values by which the highest esteem is accorded to independence, to working and earning, to individual enterprise and achievement—were richly nourished in the soil of expanding capitalism, but that their tap-root runs much deeper: deep into the past, deep into the fundamental layers of the Christian tradition of the West. It is perhaps because this tap-root remains, still powerful in nourishing our fundamental and perhaps unconscious assumptions, that the tree of values which burgeoned in an age when our economic system required an ever-increasing number of producers survives and still has life in it in an age when the economic need is not for more producers but for more consumers.

The tap-root, we have suggested, is a root of two strands: belief that the special dignity of man lies in the presence in him, marred but not effaced, of the image of God; and belief that God, in His relationship to the world, is the everlasting subject, characterized by endless activity and creativity. Now in a certain sense, as we have suggested, this concept of God is not to be disputed. The world *is* by the activity of God: but for that activity there would be no world. There is no 'mutuality' between God and the world, no mutual complementation of cause and effect. God is not passible to the world, not exposed to an other and alien source of activity. All *is* by and through the activity of God. But in reflecting on the disclosure of God which appears in Jesus, we discerned the paradoxical possibility that He Who is *non passibilis* is *passus*: that the activity of God culminates in that form of activity which creates its own passion, that form of working which destines itself to waiting. The possibility is that God Himself, of His own free initiative, 'hands Himself over', makes Himself object to the world: in loving the world gives to the world the terrible power to have meaning to and for Himself. So He Who made, and everlastingly makes, the world also, of His own freedom, waits upon the world, exposed to and receptive of its power meaning. In all the history of the world *Deus, qui non passibilis, passus est.*

If this is true, it creates, as it were, a new component in that image of God which man believes himself to bear. That image must include not only activity but also exposure. Man

111

must see his dignity not only in being a point of activity in the world but also in being a point of receptivity: not only in his manifold capacity for action but also in the many facets of his passibility: not only in his potential for 'doing' but also in his exposure to 'being done to'. He must not see it as degrading that he should wait upon the world, be helped, be provided for, be dependent; for as such he is, by God's gift, what God Himself makes Himself to be. That man is made, by God's gift, to know and feel his dependence on the world is no less a mark of God's image in him than that he is made, also by God's gift, to know and feel his capacity for acting and achieving.

To man as he waits the world discloses its power of meaning—discloses itself in its heights and its depths, as wonder and terror, as blessing and threat. Man becomes, so to speak, the sharer with God of a secret—the secret of the world's power of meaning. The world is for him no mere succession of images recorded and registered in the brain: it is what Blake saw in his tiger and Kant in the starry heavens—a wonderful terror or a terrifying wonder. Rarely does man rise to such intense receptivity; but even in quite ordinary moments he becomes a point at which something in the world is not only registered but understood, experienced, recognized. Because man is in the world there are points in the world at which things no longer merely exist but are understood, appreciated, welcomed, feared, felt. Man as he waits upon the world becomes a place where the world is received not as it is received by a camera or a tape-recorder but rather with the power of meaning with which it is received by God.

We referred in an earlier chapter to an image stored in the memory: the image of a man of great achievement lying, at the end of his life, blind, immobile and almost totally helpless upon his bed. He was lying in the very room which he had planned and created to be his writing-room during his retirement. That he was not able to write and contribute to the world's store of wisdom is loss to many; but the effect that his writing might have had was perhaps no greater thing than what was actually happening in the room in which he lay.

The world might have been affected by his writings, changed in some degree for the better; but there in the room the world was being, in a profound sense of the word, *understood*. A man was there handed over to receive, without possibility of escape or evasion and scarcely any possibility of response, the impact of whatever features of the world might fall upon him—arthritic pain in its onset or easing, warmth or coolness as the sun shone through the window or passed behind a cloud, the sound of wind in the trees or voices from another room: food from his wife's hands, her almost constant presence, her occasional absence: a visit from a friend and whatever the friend might say: the failure of another friend to come. 'How much', one would be inclined to say, 'these things must have meant to him'; and in saying this one would put one's finger rather precisely on the 'greatness' of what was happening in the room. Variations of sun and shade, voices and passing sounds, were raised to a kind of greatness in that room because they bore with unmitigated intensity upon a figure totally exposed to them. That figure was a point at which ordinary events became exceedingly important not for their material consequences but for the appearance in and to that figure of their power of meaning.

In a radio receiver radio waves are transformed into audible sounds. Without the receiver the waves exist merely as waves: in and through the receiver there is actualized their potential for becoming sounds. One might use the radio receiver as an analogy of the transforming power of man's receptivity of the world. Without that receptivity the world exists simply as physical fact: in and through man's receptivity there is actualized its potential for becoming wonder and terror, promise and threat, pleasure and pain, beauty and squalor. Beauty, as opposed to physical fact, appears within the world when a butterfly's wing is seen by a human eye and when its potential for beauty is actualized in a human mind. So when a man receives and recognizes the beauty of a butterfly's wing he is no less enriching the totality of the world than when, by art and skill, he creates—if that were possible—a thing of equal beauty. A man who receives and recognizes the beauty of a garden is no less enriching the totality of the world than a man who works upon and creates a garden.

From the standpoint of the Christian faith, the potential of the world for beauty and squalor, for wonder and terror, for many shades and varieties of meaning, is an authentic potential—as authentic as the potential of radio waves to become sounds. Beauty and squalor and other varieties of meaning are not merely projected upon the world by man's imagination; for the Creator Himself has given to the world not only power of being but also power of meaning, not only existence but meaningful existence. So man, in perceiving meaning in the world, perceives what is really there. He sees—no doubt in a distorted or limited way—what God sees: at least he sees the dimension—the dimension of meaning—which God sees. He becomes a point at which God's perception of the world is, as it were, caught in a tiny mirror and projected back to God; so that, if a flight of imagination may be permitted, God sees before Him not only the world which He has made in all its depth of meaning but also myriads of points at which something of that depth of meaning is received by human consciousness and reflected back to Him. God creates a world which includes among its infinite variety of wonders this culminating wonder—that there are points within it at which, in the consciousness of men, its wonders are received and recognized.

In recent theological thinking much has been made of man's role in sharing or even extending the creativity of God. Man has been seen, primarily, as 'fellow-worker with God'— as participator, albeit on a humble scale, in God's everlasting activity of remaking and redeeming the world. Perhaps this understanding of man's role needs to be balanced by the perception of man as 'fellow receiver with God'. The phrase is unfamiliar and inelegant; and, strictly speaking, it would be correct to use instead the more familiar phrase 'fellow-sufferer with God'. But the word 'suffer' has come to have over the years an ever narrower connotation, and its associations are now restricted to 'pain', 'hardship', 'distress'. It is in a much wider sense than this that man is fellow-sufferer

114

with God. He is one who, like God, is handed over to the world, to wait upon it, to receive its power of meaning: to be the one upon whom the world bears in all its variety and intensity of meaning: to receive upon his transforming consciousness no mere photographic imprint of the world but its wonder and terror, its vastness and delicacy, its beauty and squalor, its good and evil. It is in this dimension—the dimension of meaning—that man receives the world; and as he does so, a figure exposed and waiting, he appears no diminished or degraded figure but a figure of enormous dignity. As he waits in the future, increasingly dependent on systems and machines, on organization and technology, on medical support and social provision, he will in no sense be deprived of his high calling—that of standing beside God and receiving into the transforming mirror of his consciousness what the world really is. Whenever he so stands, in the future as in the past and present, man will be a figure of unique and almost unbelievable dignity.